PSYCHE'S
STORIES

PSYCHE'S STORIES

Modern Jungian Interpretations of Fairy Tales

EDITED BY MURRAY STEIN AND LIONEL CORBETT

Volume Two

CHIRON PUBLICATIONS
WILMETTE, ILLINOIS

Library of Congress Catalog Card Number: 90-26108

Printed in the United States of America.
Copyediting and book design by Siobhan Drummond.
Original art by Drev Sine and Treehaus.

Library of Congress Cataloging-in-Publication Data:
(Revised for volume 2)
Psyche's stories.
    Includes bibliographical references.
    1. Fairy tales – History and criticism. 2. Jung,
C. G. (Carl Gustav), 1875-1961. 3. Psychoanalysis
and folklore. 3. Archetype (Psychology) I. Stein,
Murray, 1943-   . II. Corbett, Lionel.
GR550.P78 1991   398′.019   90-26108
ISBN 0-933029-39-X (v. 1)
ISBN 0-933029-56-X (v. 2)

Contents

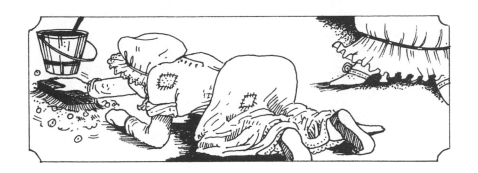

"Maid Maleen"
An Image of Feminine Wholeness

Frances M. Parks

When I first read the Grimms' fairy tale, "Maid Maleen" (1819), I felt that it was a story about me and about many women I have known in my analytic practice. I will look at it as a story that reflects processes involved in a woman achieving a sense of her own identity, her sense of self. Obviously women find various paths on this journey, but for many women periods of depression and feelings of isolation are experiences along the way. This story offers images useful in relating to and giving meaning to such episodes of depression. In the figure of Maid Maleen we find a parallel to the modern woman who, unable to realize her own development through the collective, finds herself isolated psychologically.

Maid Maleen

T he tale opens with a prince asking for the hand of Maid Maleen, the daughter of a king. As the father of Maid Maleen wishes to give her to another, the request is refused. Maid Maleen loved the prince who had asked for her hand and refused to make the match her father wished. Enraged by his daughter's willfulness, the king ordered a tower to be built and Maid Maleen with her attendant maid to be locked away for seven years. They were given a sufficient supply of food and water. During the seven years the prince often circled around the tower calling to Maid Maleen, but no sound pierced the thick walls.

As the supply of food and water began to run low, Maid Maleen and her attendant realized that the seven years were ending, but no one came to rescue them. In order to avoid a miserable death, the two women started to work to bore through the walls. Finally they escaped, only to discover that the kingdom had been at war and all signs of life had been destroyed. They then started on a journey to a new country, eating nettles to survive.

Arriving at last in a new country, they looked many places but discovered that work was hard to find. Eventually they were allowed to become scullery maids in the kitchen of the royal palace. This was the palace of the prince who had loved Maid Maleen. The father of the prince had chosen a new bride for his son and preparations were being made for the wedding.

The intended bride was ugly and did not want her ugliness to be seen in public. She tried to persuade Maid Maleen to stand in for her at the wedding. Maid Maleen at first refused; the ugly bride then threatened that such an attitude would cost Maid Maleen her life. So the wedding occurred with Maid Maleen in the place of the ugly bride. As the prince led her to the church, Maid Maleen spoke to the nettle plant and recalled the eating of this plant on the journey. She spoke to the bridge and to the church door asking that they not break, which would suggest that she was not the true bride. Before entering the church, the prince placed a precious chain around the neck of Maid Maleen.

That evening in the bridal chamber, the prince asked the ugly bride about the words spoken on the way to the church. When she could not answer, the deception of the ugly bride and the true identity of Maid Maleen were revealed. The ugly bride was beheaded; Maid Maleen and the prince kissed "and were happy all the days of their lives."

DEFIANCE OF THE FATHER

The story begins with the king who is powerful and presumes to dictate the course of his daughter's life. The king, who represents the collective cultural values, has no tolerance for wishes at variance with his own. The patriarchy is quite willing to define the course of our lives unless we choose to take a conscious and individual stand. In our modern culture we take for granted that a woman may choose a wedding partner, but to have the awareness, strength, and courage to live an individual life (married or not) is problematic for most of us. Such an individual stance may be expressed when women, for their own development, make a decision to withdraw to a cloistered religious life or to a cabin in the woods or to enter analysis to do their own inner psychological work. More often, the decision is not a conscious one, and women are likely to feel that a separateness or isolation is imposed upon them. Then the reaction may be one of depression and despair.

A lovely image of a woman finding the true self through acting in her own individual way is that of Mary Magdalene. Her love of Christ led her to anoint his feet with oil. In this act, she defied the bounds by which her culture defined her and she was transformed. As Maleen is a variation of the name Magdalene, it is likely that there are some parallels between the two images.

The king's reaction to his daughter's wish for self-determination is to imprison her with her attendant in a dark tower for seven years in an effort to break her "perverse spirit." In the tower, the women are cut off from the sky and from the earth; when we are separated from father sky and mother earth, life energy is held in abeyance. We are told that Maid Maleen and her attendant could do nothing but "lament and complain." In working with depressed patients, I am often amazed, and encouraged, at the amount of energy that can be summoned in the service of complaining. Initially, Maid Maleen and her attendant are power-less and must submit to a situation imposed on them. I think it is significant that they are not so powerless after seven years have passed!

And so they wait. The tower is a symbol with multiple meanings. In some contexts it may convey the idea of elevation or ascent, although here the image is more one of confinement and darkness. The tower connotes transformation and evolution (Cirlot 1962). Cooper (1978) suggests that when the tower holds a virgin or princess it takes on the significance of an enclosed space or walled garden, again a place of transformation, of growth – a womb.

What is the quality of time in the tower? There is light from neither sun nor moon. Depression often alters the quality of time, and the body seems disconnected from the normal day/night cycle. In many fairy tales, the waiting princess is given a task of weaving, sorting, etc., but such is not the case here. It is a black time, a time only for waiting. The growth or transformation is on an unconscious level, and the conscious feeling may be only boredom or lament. It is dark in the womb and in the winter earth. Nor Hall writes of "spiritual pregnancy": "pregnancy is a nocturnal mystery characterized by hiddenness, veiling, submission, waiting, regenerative growth, inner harmony" (1980, p. 95). She speaks of the need for withdrawal and isolation as a prerequisite for creativity.

In a discussion of the difference between patriarchal and matriarchal consciousness, Neumann states:

> While patriarchal consciousness annihilates time and outstrips nature's slow process of transformation and evolution by its purposive use of experiment and calculation, matriarchal consciousness remains caught in the spell of the changing moon. Like the moon, its illumination and its luminosity are bound to the flow of time and to periodicity. It must wait for time to ripen, while with time, like sown seed, comprehension ripens too. . . .Only when the time is "fulfilled" does understanding come as an illumination. (1973, pp. 46–47)

I would suggest that this period of isolation and waiting is the critical incident in this tale, as such a period may be in a woman's development. Discussion of this problem is a major theme in Marie-Louise von Franz's series of lectures published as *The Feminine in Fairytales* (1974). She gives many examples of the woman retiring to the forest or having to wait for a particular phase of the moon. In a discussion of "The Handless Maiden," she says:

> for many years the woman drifted more and more out of life and was cured only by accepting the fact that she had to stay quiet in the woods, and temporarily not go back into life. This is a very frequent motif, and being excluded from life for many years seems to me typically to illustrate a problem of feminine psychology. From the outside it looks like complete stagnation, but in reality it is a time of initiation and incubation when a deep inner split is cured and inner problems solved. This motif forms a contrast to the more active quest of the male hero, who has to go into the Beyond and try to slay the monster, or to find the treasure or the bride. Usually he has to make more of a journey and accomplish some deed instead of just staying out of life. There seems to be a typical difference between the masculine and feminine principle, the latter being the more passive. The unconscious is experienced as isolation and afterwards comes the return into life. (von Franz 1974, p. 94)

She suggests that such a withdrawal to the "unhurt virgin ground in her soul" is the required healing process for the woman injured by the negative animus or negative mother-complex (ibid., p. 95). Related to an example of such a process, von Franz states: "She has first to reach the zero point and then in complete loneliness find her own spiritual experience" (ibid., p. 86).

A part of most initiation rites or *rites de passage* is a period of withdrawal or isolation before the symbolic rebirth. Victor Turner (1967), in his study of initiation rites, described a middle stage which he called the "liminal period." This liminal period occurs between the initial separation from the group and the final aggregation. The isolation in the tower represents such a time. In this stage, the initiate is often treated as an embryo or newborn, or perhaps as dead. Previous identities and structures are dissolved. It is a condition of "ambiguity and paradox" (Turner 1967, p. 97). It is a time of reflection. In some cases the initiate is sequestered, as in the Hopi *kiva*, and in others the time is spent in the wilderness. The occurrence of a vision, a birth from the unconscious, is anticipated as a part of such an incubation period.

Traditionally, initiations occur at critical developmental stages. Maid Maleen is in the transition to adulthood. In his essay, "The Meaning of Depression at Significant Stages of Life," V. Walter Odajnyk (1987) suggests that depressions are a natural and meaningful part of the transition process. The transition by intent or natural process involves an undoing of the conscious psychic structure which may lead to an encounter with the unconscious. Odajnyk develops Jung's idea that in its natural condition, the unconscious is in a depressed state. When ego-consciousness experiences an awareness of the power of the unconscious, reactions of depression or mania are not unusual. The depressive reaction is characterized by loss of energy and darkness; it is expressed in alchemical language by the *nigredo* (blackening) which was the first stage in the alchemical work. *Nigredo* was associated with the melancholic temperament; it was a quality of the *prima materia*, the chaotic, the unformed. Odajnyk states:

> The "nigredo" therefore leads to an encounter with the shadow and then with the animus and the anima, initially in their black, unredeemed, unconscious state. If the conscious mind allows itself to be influenced by these figures, it must inevitably become infected with their blackness and turn melancholic. But that is exactly how

they are redeemed and made less black, while the conscious mind
becomes less clear and bright, and less cheerful. (1987, p. 350)

Two examples from my analytic practice remind me of
women in this kind of dark isolation. The first, whom I shall call
Susan, had enjoyed a successful career in the academic world. She
had been an effective and admired teacher and had an impressive
resume of publications and presentations. At age thirty-seven,
she was married to a man whom she loved very much. Much to
her dismay, following the marriage she experienced a block which
made academic writing almost impossible. With this interruption
in her professional skills came attacks of self-criticism, anxiety,
and depression. By external standards things had gone well for
Susan as long as she had devoted her energy to please the patriarchy of academia. The decision, however, to live out aspects of
her feminine side brought despair and suffering. Her conscious
wish to continue work that had been important to her seemed
powerless in the face of an unknown and hence frightening force.
"It" seemed to control her life. Good conscious intentions to continue work on a research project led mainly to frustration.
Months of analytic work facilitated the connection with positive
aspects of the animus. New attitudes of trust and of the valuing
of feminine aspects of the psyche emerged; judgments made with
feeling could be as respected as those made by thinking. Energy
gradually returned; with it came productive work and ideas for
new directions.

The second woman, here called Laura, had devoted the first
twenty years of her adult life to a marriage and family, feeling
that she would find an identity for herself if she could create the
model, happy, harmonious picture-book family. Needless to say,
children and husband did not cooperate, and there were problems
not unlike those of most modern families. Now with children out
of the house and feeling some sense of failure at not producing the
model "happy family," she had to face having spent many years
trying to meet expectations that she felt would gain her acceptance in the eyes of others and that her own sense of self had been
lost somewhere along the way. The first stage in her own development was one of feeling very isolated and depressed. Working
with fabrics and weaving eventually helped her to see some of the
unique patterns in her own life and development.

For each of these women there was a long period of frustration, and there were feelings of detachment, isolation, and of

depression. Such periods are so uncomfortable it is not surprising that one cannot easily remain patient. At such times trying to "do" more just makes things worse.

Similarly, the discomfort touches complexes of those around us in such ways that they in all good faith feel a need to offer solutions. During the time that Maid Maleen and her attendant were in the tower, the king's son went around the tower and called their names, but "no sound pierced through the dark walls." Here is a vivid picture of the ineffectiveness of external intervention on this kind of psychic withdrawal or isolation. Thus when one is in such a state, another's counsel to "take a trip" or "do some volunteer work" or "take up painting" has no effect. The medical profession offers a plethora of pills for quick relief; these effects are often, at best, temporary.

Seven years pass and the food supply runs low; Maid Maleen fears that she and her attendant have been forgotten. The number seven occurs in many contexts to suggest intervals of significant change. For the human fetus, seven months is considered the age of "viability." At that time, all organs have been formed, and although uterine growth is not complete, the organism can survive in the outside world. A unique new and viable structure has been formed in the darkness of the womb. Seven is the number of the creation myth in Genesis. In the story, "The Handless Maiden," the young woman remained in isolation in the forest for seven years. It is during this time that she was renewed; her own hands grew back again. In discussing the parallel in psychic development, Julia Jewett (1987) states:

> At this stage, what is to be made is a Self. At this stage we realize that everything we are about is "not" to gratify the ego—"not" to look good in the world or to make money or something, but the life work of creating the Self that we are, that we will be, and that ultimately needs to be of the durability that will get it across the threshold called death. That is the great transition. (p. 171)

> This seven-year stretch in the woods is a period of deep introversion which is absolutely necessary to really get to the bottom of things, to really know oneself. And then she grows her own hands. She will have her own ground, her own standpoint, her own style, her own Self. (p. 172)

Now for first time in our story, Maid Maleen takes an active, conscious, thinking stance and uses the bread knife to break through the wall. Had she remained eternally in her passive, unconscious, feminine state, she would have perished. And so after seven years in the tower, she and her maid emerge through the opening they have cut. She is reborn.

The work to make the opening takes three days. We are reminded that three is a dynamic number pointing toward, but not having reached, completion. She and her attendant emerge into a wasteland, her father's kingdom having been destroyed. Perhaps this destruction occurred because the feminine had not been honored. (That is the other side of the story from the masculine point of view.)

Both Susan and Laura experienced much distress when what had been valued parts of their lives ceased to provide meaning. Tasks into which they had invested so much energy now seemed empty and irrelevant; what previously was important now seemed a wasteland. This episode in the story would suggest that just to wait for the dark to pass and for growth and transformation to occur in the unconscious may not be sufficient; there may remain work to be done on another level. Transformation and psychic change do not move according to a consciously planned timetable. I am reminded of a patient who after several months of work would say to me and to God: "Ok, I've suffered enough, isn't it time for a change?" And when the change comes, it may not be what we might have wished.

JOURNEY TO A NEW LAND

Maid Maleen and her attendant cannot find shelter or food and are forced to "appease their hunger with nettles." Nettles tend to grow in wastelands and at waysides, reminding us that nourishment can come from that which is not of obvious value. The nettle with its stinging leaves is a symbol of cruelty, but it also has been seen as a symbol of courage (Powell 1979). The nettle has medicinal uses; it is especially valuable for the treatment of anemia – it can give strength. A German man who escaped from a prisoner-of-war camp at the end of World War II told me of surviving on nettles for weeks as he attempted to travel undetected across the country. A Swiss man told me that he uses the plant to make a liquid fertilizer for his garden each spring. The nettle becomes an interesting symbol for the gifts from mother earth; it is a plant that can bring pain and can also give nourishment. The way for

Maid Maleen continues to be one of suffering and poverty, but with an aspect of nourishment and growth.

WORK IN THE KITCHEN

Finally Maid Maleen and her attendant arrive in another country, suggesting that there has been a psychological transformation, perhaps still below the level of consciousness if we draw the parallel to personal development. After long searching to find work, they are given jobs as scullery maids in the royal palace. There is hard work to be done. Work in the kitchen is feminine, creative work whether done by a man or a woman. It reminds us of all the rich symbols from alchemy of preparation, sorting, combining, cooking, and transformation. To clean and prepare fresh vegetables, to smell garlic on our fingers, provides for many of us at least brief connections with mother earth as we live busy lives in concrete cities. Scullery work is hard, and it is work done by our bodies and not our heads. In a depression, one feels isolated from one's body as well as from everything else. Physical activity often provides the first break in a period of depression. Such work can take varied forms. It might be effort in the kitchen or yard, or swimming or brisk walking along the forest path, but it must be done as serious work.

The king has chosen for his son another bride. Because of her ugliness, the new bride shuts herself in her room and there Maid Maleen carries to her meals from the kitchen. The ugly bride is fearful of being seen, and so, with dire threats, she insists that Maid Maleen take her place in the wedding. Maid Maleen at first refuses, stating: "I wish for no honor which is not suitable for me." The ugly bride here is like the witch or false bride in other stories. She is an aspect of the dark mother who would destroy all for her own benefit. She is not unlike the king at the beginning of the tale who is interested only in his own needs or fulfillment of his own wishes. We can also see the ugly bride as undeveloped psychologically. She is willing to play a role prescribed for her by others; she has not made the effort to become conscious and differentiated. She does not know or trust herself. When questioned by the king's son later in the tale, she must seek answers from her maid, "who keeps my thoughts for me."

I know in myself, and have seen in analysands, the frustrations and disappointment when, after long efforts to be aware and to know our shadows, complexes of greed and envy erupt, threatening to destroy everything. The ugly bride represents such a complex. We may be aware that a complex like this is quite irrational but that does not diminish its power. It is a devouring monster that will destroy what we love most and will leave us hurt and alone. If we can hold on and not act out the destructiveness, it may be possible to find aspects of our own loveliness, creativity, or brightness which have been undeveloped in our selves and therefore projected onto others.

In reading the fairy tale we might question at this point why Maid Maleen did not take an active stand against the ugly bride and claim her rightful place as the beloved of the prince. Perhaps her experience of waiting and of suffering has enabled her to trust in a process other than that of rational control.

THE WEDDING

As the king's son leads Maid Maleen to the church, she speaks to the nettle plant, the foot bridge, and the church door. Her way to the church reflects her path of development. She passes the nettle, a reminder of her suffering and need but also of her connection with the earth. The foot bridge is the transition from one state to another leading to the church, the symbol of spiritual wholeness. Maid Maleen now appears to be firmer in her own identity, stating to the bridge and church door, "I am not the true bride," but the other part of her statement, "Do not break," would suggest that for the time she is not ready for her true self to be revealed. At the church door, the king's son places a precious chain around her neck. In the church, the priest joins their hands and they are married.

The chain is a symbol of unity and matrimony. It represents "diversity in unity" as individual parts unite to make a whole (Cooper 1978). In the tale, the chain and the marriage suggest psychic bonding and integration. It is the symbol of a new and publicly acknowledged identity. We are reminded of the words in the traditional wedding ceremony: "Those whom God hath joined together. . . ." While we easily see the positive aspects of the archetype of unity, it is useful to be also aware that such an image implies being bound, chained, yoked, fettered (Hillman 1980). It implies a commitment, obligation to one direction or set of values. Such a commitment in one direction means a willingness to sacrifice various other alternatives and possibilities. When mature choices are made the unlimited possibilities of youth cease to exist. In the work of individuation, the conscious awareness of disparate parts uniting is the culmination of a long process; when this integration occurs, one's way of being is altered.

Upon returning home, Maid Maleen takes off the magnificent clothes and jewels and dresses herself in her gray gown, keeping nothing "but the jewel on her neck, which she had received from the bridegroom." The grey gown symbolizes an acknowledgment of the modest and ordinary self; Maid Maleen knows these aspects of herself because of her suffering and work. Returning to this state is a reminder that even as one comes out of a depression and is granted a glimpse of a higher level of development, there are times of regression. Also it suggests that concomitant with greater psychic development comes greater humility.

Upon questioning by the king's son regarding what had been said to the nettle, bridge, and church door on the way to the church, the ugly bride cannot reply. She has not been through the process of suffering and development. After receiving the correct answers from Maid Maleen, she orders Maid Maleen beheaded. As the servants attempt to drag her away, Maid Maleen screams loudly so that the king's son comes and orders her freed. She is now clearly willing to take an active stance to save herself – she knows and values herself. The king's son sees the gold chain and they are reunited.

This tale offers an interesting contrast to the familiar ones where the prince must go on journeys and through trials to find the princess or treasure. There is much less overt action in this story. I would suggest that the more active process may represent a typical masculine development. The development in this story comes through a time of passivity and waiting. Background work, a kind of foundation, must be made before it is possible for a balanced unity between feminine and masculine or the female psyche and animus to develop. This kind of depression, inactivity, and inward turning are difficult for us to tolerate in a world that values extroversion and activity. We fear aloneness and solitude.

Both Susan and Laura continue to work, each in her individual way moving toward psychic union. Both women showed courage and faith in living out months filled mainly with depression and despair. Both were willing to work in areas that were personally difficult.

The woman who develops consciousness out of her own darkness and suffering remains virginal in the sense of being truly individual and not obtaining her identity through identification with another, whether that be another person or her work. This image of virginity (which is unrelated to sexual chasteness or lack thereof) reflects the transformation of the basic instinct for union with the mother into a desire for spiritual unity with the soul. This is the process of individuation. Like other archetypal processes, it is reflected, at least partially, in diverse images. It is solitary Artemis; it is Persephone hidden away in the underworld; it is Demeter wandering alone, searching in grief for her lost daughter; it is Joseph waiting in prison in Egypt; it is Mary waiting with her cousin Elizabeth and again waiting at the foot of the cross; it is Mary Magdalene who provides us with a beautiful example of individuation out of love. It is the Buddha beneath the Bo tree. The process of feminine individuation is suggested in the simple title of this fairy tale. Although, on one level, the story is about a marriage, it is also about a holy, psychic union, and the heroine is virginal, a maiden: she is not called a princess or a queen, she is Maid Maleen.

REFERENCES

Cirlot, J. D. 1962. *A Dictionary of Symbols*. London: Routledge and Kegan Paul.

Cooper, J. C. 1978. *An Illustrated Encyclopedia of Traditional Symbols*. London: Thames and Hudson.

Grimm, J. and Grimm W. 1819. *The Complete Grimm's Fairy Tales*. New York: Pantheon Books, 1944.

Hall, N. 1980. *The Moon and the Virgin*. London: The Women's Press.

Hillman, J. 1980. On the necessity of abnormal psychology: Ananke and Athene. In *Facing the Gods*. Dallas: Spring Publications.

Jewett, J. 1987. Womansoul: a feminine corrective to Christian imagery. In Stein, M., Moore, R. L., eds., *Jung's Challenge to Contemporary Religion*. Wilmette, Ill.: Chiron Publications.

Neumann, E. 1973. The moon and matriarchal consciousness. In Hillman, J., et al., *Fathers and Mothers*. Zurich: Spring Publications.

Odajnyk, V. W. 1987. The meaning of depression at significant stages of life. In Mahdi, L. D.; Foster, S.; and Little, M., eds., *Betwixt and Between: Patterns of Masculine and Feminine Initiation*. LaSalle, Ill.: Open Court.

Powell, C. 1979. *The Meaning of Flowers*. Boulder, Colo.: Shambhala
    Press.
Turner, V. 1967. *The Forest of Symbols*. Ithaca, N.Y.: Cornell University
    Press.
von Franz, M.-L. 1974. *The Feminine in Fairytales*. Zurich: Spring Publi-
    cations.

"The Old Woman in the Wood"

Caroline Stevens

Quite often now, she visits our dreams:

> *An Old Woman delivers a package, but it is not what the dreamer ordered. When the "delivery woman" insists, the dreamer flies into a rage and attacks her. The Old Woman is transformed, becomes grotesquely serpentine, writhing and mocking.*

> *The dreamer performs before an audience of men, flying, circling like a ferris wheel. Below her on the floor sits an Old Woman. The dreamer says something insulting, patronizing, and the Old Woman becomes a snarling cat who rises to do combat, disrupting the dreamer's airy performance.*

> *In the initial dream of analysis, a door opens, and an Old Woman enters. She is unkempt, her hair disheveled, but the dreamer knows she is a successful psychic. The Old Woman comes close, and the dreamer recoils in disgust from the smell of her breath.*

Who is this Old Woman, often so unwelcome, who comes to us in the dark of night? Many variations on the theme of the ancient, lone, and lowly woman appear in the dreams of contemporary women. She may be "disadvantaged": living in a room no bigger than a closet; speaking or weeping in church, but unheard by the priest and congregation; delivering "orders" from a source unknown to the dreamer. The dreamer's ego position is "above" these manifestations, and she may feel compassion for the "poor old lady." But when such a figure suggests or reveals power, the ego often reacts with fear or anger.

It seems that there is an Old Woman who will no longer simply wait for us, as once did the witch far away in the depths of a forest. She has become insistent, importunate. Once upon a time, her stories were told and her power was known. But that power has been very long in the shadows, more feared than respected when it was known, and lately, very little known. Only now, disturbed in our dreams, do we begin again to ponder the stories.

The Old Woman in the Wood

A poor servant girl was traveling with the family she served, and the road took them through the depths of a great forest. Deep in the woods, they were set upon by robbers. Terrified, the servant girl jumped out of the carriage and hid herself behind a tree, while the robbers killed everyone they found and rode off with the family's wealth. When they had gone, the girl found herself alone and abandoned, the sole witness to a dreadful carnage. She wept and wrung her hands and wondered: "What can a poor girl like me do now? I do not know my way, and no human help is at hand. Surely I will starve, or be eaten by wild animals."

Nevertheless, she tried her best to find a road, running this way and that, until at last she was exhausted. Then she sat down under a tree, and gave herself into God's keeping, resolving to stay where she was and accept her fate. So she sat and she waited, and after a while, a white dove came flying down out of the trees with a little golden key in its beak. It put the little key in her hand, and showed her the great tree that the key would open. Inside the tree, the girl found a little dish of milk and plenty of good white bread, and she ate her fill. Then she was overcome with weariness and longed for sleep.

Now the dove flew to her again, with another golden key in its bill, and in a second great tree the girl found a clean white bed. There she lay down and slept, and woke refreshed. In the morning the dove came again with a key. Once again the key opened a tree, and inside this third tree the servant girl found beautiful clothing woven of silk and of gold, garments fit for the daughter of a king.

And so the girl lived for some time in the woods, the dove supplying all of her needs, and her life there was happy and serene.

Then one day the dove came and asked if she would do something for him, and the girl, full of gratitude, was glad to reply, "With all my heart." Now the dove told her that an old woman lived in the woods, and she must go to her house to find something of great value. He would show her the way, but then she must enter the house, passing by the old woman on the right side and giving no answer to her greeting. Inside the house she would find a room overflowing with gems and bejewelled rings, but she should seek out only one, a plain gold ring, and bring it back to the dove with all possible speed.

The girl went to the little house and came to the door. There sat an old woman who stared when she saw her, but greeted her kindly: "Good day, my child." But the girl gave no answer and opened the door of the old woman's house. The old woman cried "Stop!" and grabbed at her gown. "This is my house," she said, "where no one can enter if I choose not to allow it." Still the girl said nothing, but went into the house and found her way to the room full of rings. She was dazzled by the beauty there and searched in vain through the glittering gems for a plain gold ring. But while she was seeking, she saw the old woman stealing away, holding a bird cage in her hand. The girl followed after and took the cage from the old woman's hand. When she looked closely, she saw that a bird was inside the cage, and in the bird's bill was the plain gold ring that she sought. And away she ran then with the ring, full of joy, expecting to find the little white dove awaiting her return.

But he was not there, and so once again she leaned against a tree and waited. As she leaned there, the tree grew soft and bent its branches down, and they became two arms that held her. When she looked round, she saw no tree, but a handsome man, who kissed her and told her that she had freed him from enchantment. The old woman, he said, was a wicked witch, whose power had changed him into a tree. Every day for two hours he became a white dove, but as long as the old woman had the ring, he could not become again a human man. Now all his servants and horses, who had also been changed into trees, were released from the old woman's spell, and he led them all forth to his kingdom. For he was a king's son, and he and the girl were soon married and lived happily.

We will certainly reflect a bit on the "happy ending," so familiar to all of us from song and story and cinema, if not so common now as it once was, in fiction or in fact. (How common it may ever have been in fact, of course, is rather difficult to say.) However, let's first see what insights this tale may give us, for it seems to be, more clearly than most fairy tales, a statement about feminine development toward psychic wholeness.

At the beginning of this tale, retold by the Brothers Grimm, we find depicted a quite contemporary state of the soul, most particularly of many a woman on entering analysis. Like the servant girl, she has been in service to "a family," her identity and status derived from that experience. The family has defined and contained her: first, the family of her origin which taught her what she might be and hope to become as a woman, and then, perhaps, a family in which she has been wife and mother. But something has assailed the status quo, has deprived her of all comfort and satisfaction she may have felt in the roles she has played.

Perhaps her outer circumstances have been attacked (by the loss of a job, her husband's infidelity, the children's approaching adulthood). But often there is nothing external which might explain her feelings of unrest, confusion, depression. Something profoundly disruptive has occurred deep in the forest of the unconscious. In our story, violent shadow figures have emerged and robbed the servant girl of her accustomed source of place and value. And she does not know where she is, nor how to find her way further. Even the road which brought her to this place is gone. There is no going back.

The dark and mysterious forest has long been a symbol of the unconscious. Here is nature uncultivated and uncontrolled by human law and conscious effort, where animals, birds, and growing things of all kinds live according to organically evolved laws of their own and Mother Nature. And here is a refuge for all that rejects and is rejected by the collective – a natural haunt for robbers, for men who do not follow the rules or fill the roles of society (von Franz 1980, p. 52). They kill and rob in a pitiless way, but by doing so, they bring the servant girl of our story into fuller relationship with the unconscious, depriving her at once of all possibility of reliance on her prior position and relation to her old, conscious attitudes.

In her treatment of the robber band in the *Golden Ass*, Marie-Louise von Franz suggests, in fact, that robbers may function as the servants of the Mother Goddess, like the Kuretes, Satyri, and Kabiri which surrounded the figure of the Goddess in ancient Greece and Asia Minor (ibid., p. 53). They were guardians of the Divine Child – of the Self – and they also represented a kind of chthonic male virility, madness, and creativity. In our story we can regard them as revealing the collective shadow, the dark and violent shadow of patriarchy. But they also represent the servant girl's first contact with her own animus, multiple as newly emerging figures may be, contaminated by her own as well as by collective shadow contents.

Indeed, these robbers image the very qualities which women must most desperately repress and deny in order to maintain an acceptable feminine persona. The robbers take rather than give; in fact, they are willing to do harm in order to get what they want. They deal death rather than life and nurture, and they do not serve the family: they destroy it. Although these qualities are certainly shadowy for men, and may be indulged only "in a good cause," they are oddly also often qualities which belong to heroes. But women are likely to feel such qualities as quite totally other, impossible in themselves. And so, in a woman's dream, her rage, her aggressive capacities, her will to violence, her greed, are likely to appear in masculine form, and to accomplish the very loss she fears they will in the day world: the loss of her place and her role and the presence of others on whom to depend.

Such animus figures are often, in our culture's time and space, a necessary mediator to the deeper levels of femininity, to the Feminine Self. We know that the dark gods may play a significant role in the feminine mysteries: Hades, the lord of the underworld, carries Persephone, all unwilling, down to his realm; Psyche accepts a "marriage of death" with Amor who comes to her only in the dark of the night. And Dionysus, the "mad god," seduces away the reluctant and dutiful good women of Thebes, away from their looms and their babes, to dance with him on the wild mountainside. We may think also of Hermes, whose ambivalent character, from the standpoint of human morality, is well known in mythology. He is called the god of thieves and cheats. Yet he is also the guide of souls and the messenger of the gods, bringing us closer to their wisdom and power, closer to the Self. And as the robbers emerged from the thicket, so Hermes-Mercurius is called by Jung the "*spiritus vegetativus*," pervading nature with a power both life-giving and destructive (Jung 1954, par. 408).

However, the servant girl's first encounter with the animus, in this initial rampaging form of the robbers, is a brief and terrifying one, and she escapes from their murderous potential by hiding behind a tree – a part of the same Great Mother's forest from which they emerged. Now she is all alone, and she perceives her situation to be desperate: "What can a poor girl like me do now?" In the manner of fairy tales, not much is indicated about the suffering that comes with such an experience of loss, of isolation, of confusion. The servant girl might trust in God when she could no longer trust the outer world, but such a response is harder now. When we lose our faith in the collective, we may be lost indeed, and it is exceedingly hard to believe that this dark, abandoned place is where we simply must abide, no longer "doing," simply waiting.

Our culture's masculine ideal is surrendered here, and this can be hard and humiliating for contemporary women as well as for men. We – our conscious selves – are supposed to know what to do and how to do it, where we are, where we are going, and how to get there. And we are supposed to be able to do and be all this "independently." Although women have often believed they could and should rely on men for guidance, caring, and strength, women today, like the servant girl, may discover they cannot. Moreover, we begin to believe that we should not, that such reliance has kept us childlike and servile, and that it has burdened our relationships – and our men – with unrealistic expectations. But many women are also discovering the limits of "self"-reliance, when by that is understood a reliance upon only so much of ourselves as has become available to us, growing up female in the culture of patriarchy. Meanwhile, the Old Woman waits in the forest of the unconscious.

Von Franz has noted, in connection with the story of the Handless Maiden, that all a woman may be able to do, if she is faced with a particularly powerful negative animus, is to run away and hide, and wait in isolation from the world, wait for the strengthening of femininity which will permit a meeting with the animus without destructive possession by it (von Franz 1972, pp. 77–79). But "possession" by the masculine has been the norm in our culture, in the manner well-noted by Erich Neumann: the girl-child is enraptured and drawn away from her merger with the mother by a numinous paternal power, and only the later appearance of the hero can rescue her from the father's realm. The hero then leads her into a patriarchal marriage. But here, too, she is at risk of a kind of arrested development, and a loss of self, for the traditional "head" of the family is masculine (Neumann 1959). And the masculine authority that she has internalized in her growing-up dominates her capacity to understand and value herself. She is always placating this power, the "negative animus," who questions and criticizes and passes judgment on her every effort at thought and personal expression and initiative.

And so in some degree the hiding that von Franz suggests may be necessary is in fact a likelihood for all women, if they are to preserve the capacity for psychological growth. Something in us withdraws from the power of the father world, hides away, rests in "the woods" of the unconscious. When it can and must, it will make itself known to us, often, as in our tale, with a violence that destroys our previous adapted life. If we find then the grace and the support to wait for it, healing and transformation may begin to occur. And indeed, after the servant girl has waited "for a while," a white dove appears and provides the means to the next step: her more intimate discovery of the feminine, now more differentiated than its appearance as "the forest."

The dove has a rich symbolism. It is sometimes the symbol of John the Baptist, the herald of Christ. It appears also as the Holy Spirit, the third person of the Trinity, who brings God's grace to human beings, a messenger spirit between the servant girl's God and humanity. In this we can see the dove's relation to Hermes winged, the Greek god of thought and of revelation, who mediated between the gods of Olympus and their human worshippers. The dove has also been regarded, by the Slavs and in Roman and Visigothic art, as embodied spirit, a symbol of the human soul. And this bird is also closely associated with the Great Goddess, appearing with the love goddesses of Asia Minor, India, Crete, and Greece. We can see here, embodied in a single symbol and thus related, Logos and Eros, feminine and masculine, spirit and body.

The little key the dove brings, golden in reference to the value of what it can open, is not only phallic, masculine, but also an attribute of Hecate, the Terrible Mother, guardian of crossroads, where fateful choices are made. In the key, as throughout this tale and others, the complex and seemingly contradictory aspects of archetypes are revealed: what has seemed negative in its action, like the robbers, is necessary and in fact furthers the development of the servant girl; what appears positive, the golden key to survival and growth, reminds us nevertheless of its relation to the Dark.

Now a tree is opened to reveal the nourishing aspect of the Mother, and it is significant that the food appears in a small dish, emphasizing the position of the girl at this stage as a child relating to her mother, and that it is in the form of bread and milk. Milk is, of course, the earliest nourishment from the mother, essential to the infant's survival, and so fundamental that it is also related to Sophia, the "highest" form of the feminine, as the nourishment of philosophical wisdom which she offers. Bread, as the product of grain and again one of the most basic of foods, is intimately associated with the Mother Goddess Demeter and her counterparts the world over.

The dove then brings a second key, which opens the sheltering and transforming aspects of the Mother. Within the womb of the tree mother, the girl lies down to sleep. Her sleep there, on a clean white bed, and awakening to daylight, is like a ritual of death and rebirth, and the fact of her transformation through it is then revealed by the opening of the third tree. Here she finds the splendid garments of a king's daughter. But though she wears the garments, she is not yet ready to act as a king's daughter, and for some time she lives a safe and happy life, relying upon the care and guidance of the dove.

Three is the dynamic number of change, and for the servant girl there have been three trees, in which she found nourishment, sleep, and transformation: life, death, and rebirth. In alchemy the tree symbolizes the opus, the work of transformation, and as in alchemy the base material is transformed into the gold of the Self, so the servant girl has become like a king's daughter. Yet the process is not complete. Something more awaits her, and one day the dove asks her to do something for his sake. The servant girl now learns from the dove about the existence and whereabouts of the Old Woman in the Wood.

In other times and places, both the light and the dark aspects of the Great Goddess have been acknowledged and symbolized. However, in Christianity, the Goddess has been neglected, the knowledge of her power remaining largely unrecognized and unexpressed, except for its spiritualized and secondary manifestations in Sophia and the Virgin Mary. Only the figure of the witch survived as the archetypal figure of the Great Mother, her power appearing primarily in its destructive aspect. That she lives deep in the forest shows her very far from the collective consciousness, and in many stories she is depicted as largely unconscious herself—as in "Hansel and Gretel" and "Jorinda and Joringel," where she is said to have red eyes that cannot see very well. In the latter story the witch's connection with the Great Goddess is shown by her ability to lure and control wild animals and birds and her propensity for assuming the shape of a cat or an owl. In "The Beautiful Wassilissa," the connection is even clearer, for the Baba Yaga speaks of her day, her night, and her sun, and she lives in a hut surrounded by a fence of human bones and skulls, again deep in a forest. There she is a goddess of day and night, of life and death, as well as of untamed nature (von Franz 1972, pp. 154–155). And now the servant girl must go herself to face the Old Woman and secure the treasure, a plain ring that she holds among many rings which are bejewelled and splendid.

Let me note again that the "robbers" were necessary to force the servant girl out of the shelter of the patriarchal family. If it is the only shelter we know, we will not willingly give it up. But it has not been an adequate shelter for the feminine soul. The ideal woman in patriarchy is valued for her service to others but denied the experience of personal authority and of values grounded in her own experience, both bodily and spiritual. Our mothers and our mothers' mothers have done their best to shape us as they were shaped, by the ideals of loving service to others; but they have not been able to value in themselves or in us, their daughters, the fullness of feminine selfhood. In patriarchy, therefore, often the only seeming source of such powerful and sustaining recognition and care has been God (the Father), or the prince, the hero of folk and fairy tale (the lover/husband).

Consider: the behavior of the dove-prince is the dream of many a woman yet today, and the quiet, good life he provides, privileged, safe and serene, is what many a woman still believes should have been her fate. As with the prince in Cinderella, or Sleeping Beauty, or Briar Rose, the timely appearance of the young king in "The Girl Without Hands" brings not only rescue and solace, but love and worldly position as well. We have begun to recognize that these "happy endings" are not enough, are not the whole story, and that is clearly so for the servant girl in the care of the dove. Theirs is not a human partnership, not yet productive in the realm of human action, and the servant is yet a girl, not yet an agent in the unfolding of her destiny. Now she is directed to a hidden source, to an action only she can take, an encounter with the Old Woman.

What cannot be provided by the personal mother must be discovered in the Great Mother, in the archetype, sometimes as mediated by mothering friends, teachers, therapists. This often requires a regression, momentary or extended, to the experience of unfulfilled need, of dependency on the constancy and fullness of another's presence and appropriate care. When the servant girl experiences her loss and abandonment, she gives herself into God's care and then is visited by the prince-dove. He functions as a positive and spiritualized animus figure, opening the way to an experience of nurture and shelter in feminine nature: her own nature and Mother Nature. There is an experience of the masculine that is responsive to her needs, and there is here, in the seeming wilderness, something to trust that is not masculine. Here we may note the potential for healing through a therapist, male or female, who can constellate such a guide to the Self. It is, I think, essential that the therapist recognize the ultimate necessity for a woman's experience of the feminine archetype of the Self.

Now, however—and characteristically, in the service of another's need—the servant girl goes to the house of the mysterious Old Woman. The encounter that follows is typical of a certain form of feminine development, in that the overt recognition of the feminine power is (at the dove's bidding) avoided. Although she knows the Old Woman is there, the servant girl acts as though she is not. She does not enter into dialogue with her and does not actively oppose her, but simply goes quietly and firmly about the business at hand. The Old Woman tells the girl (and us) that no one can enter her house unless she allows it. And when the girl is confronted with the riches of the Self and cannot find her plain and simple share in it—the plain gold ring—the Old Woman makes its location evident by an attempt to steal away, the bird cage in her hand, the bird in the cage, and the plain gold ring in the bill of the bird. Again the girl acts firmly, takes the bird cage from the hand of the Old Woman, and the ring from the bird, and returns to her rendezvous with the dove.

Before she meets her prince, her transformed animus, we can note here an initiation into womanhood that is not commonly known or celebrated among us. The healthy mother, animal or human, delights in the separate existence of her offspring, in the growth and increasing manifestation of a child's confident individuality. The archetype that informs her "right instincts" is the Great Mother, known over the world by a thousand names and appearing in our Western tale in the diminished and distant form of the Old Woman. But women in patriarchy do not easily trust themselves, or other women. They feel the feminine to be weak, inconsequential; or if powerful, then dangerous, threatening in the way that "illegitimate" powers, unregulated and unconfined by the collective, must be. Women have looked to men, therefore, for the kind of deep recognition and support they need. Often in the inevitable disillusionment to follow, they look to their children, and to the vicarious reward of mothering others, to try to get what nourishment they can. Our culture's attenuated connection to the Goddess, the archetype of the feminine Self, has too often made hungry children of our mothers, who then find it difficult to free their offspring to their individual fates.

However, even under ideal circumstances, there can be a certain unreadiness, a hesitation on the part of the child (or, quite often, of the woman) when faced with the transition from a seemingly secure dependence to separate identity. There is a yearning back toward the womb which we can experience as a paralysis induced by the "negative mother." And so a certain courage and assertiveness, a willingness to risk and perhaps to fall short, are required if we are to make this crossing to the unexplored shores of full and responsible adulthood. These have been qualities often not recognized, rarely rewarded in girls. They have been considered to be masculine qualities, and they will therefore often appear, in our dreams as in this tale, in masculine form. The capacities that enable us to claim our selves and shape our own lives are grown in the adequate shelter and nurture imaged in the three trees of our tale; the impetus to employ these capacities appears here as the dove. "For his sake" the servant girl accepts the final task: she must be willing and able to claim her selfhood. It will not be bestowed on her merely for being; she must act. If the Old Woman had been able to frighten her away, that would have shown the girl's unreadiness for an entry into the world.

When she returns to the place where she left the dove, the servant girl finds she must wait yet again. But this time the wait is short, for she has performed the task that reveals her freed "masculine" capacities. Her prince and all his resources are released from the enchantment of childhood, and together prince and princess ride out of the forest of the unconscious.

And so once again, the happy ending, which we in our time may be challenged to revise. Certain matters are left unresolved in our tale, and they are crucial to the later development of our personal stories. On the level of personal psychology, this story tells us that there is an intimate association and interaction between the development of a woman's relation to her animus (her "masculine" qualities) and the strengthening of her relation to her own feminine nature. First one and then the other is emphasized in this story, but we do not, the story tells us, strengthen one in opposition to or in contradiction of the other. Rather, the encounter with the dark and violent animus (the robber band) leads to a more direct contact with the feminine unconscious (the depths of the forest). Waiting with some confidence in that realm permits the contact with a helpful masculine spirit, still, however, as a dove, relatively unhumanized and undifferentiated. That relationship permits again a more differentiated and positive relation to the feminine (the nourishing, sheltering, and transforming trees), which in its turn prepares the girl to hear and respond, with a whole heart, to the plea of the animus for freedom. But it is noteworthy how much of this story takes place "out of sight." All of the action takes place in the forest, much of the transformation process takes place in trees, and the girl does not see the final transformation of the king's son or realize at first what she has been able to accomplish.

It is especially significant that there is no recognition on the girl's part of the reality of the Old Woman's power, except as a power to hold and enchant, as reported by the prince, and no real confrontation with this darkness as it might relate to her own shadow and her own power. Moreover, although he tells us he had been changed into a tree by the "wicked witch," we are left to wonder how, unless she had permitted it, he became each day the dove who was able to contact the girl and give her the key to her transformation. Yet it seems clear that in the forest of the unconscious, unpersonified in part but powerful nevertheless, the Great Goddess, the feminine Self of the servant girl, has been the instigator and controller of the whole adventure. It is all her doing: her robbers, her trees, her keys, and even her dove. But the servant girl remains unaware of her own connection to the Old Woman, for it is mediated always by the masculine, and the power she holds to free or to bind is defined by the masculine as, only, "wicked." He is, as he was, a "king's son," but the girl, as his bride, remains unaware of herself as a "queen's daughter." In psychological terms, such a woman remains subordinate to the masculine powers, values them in herself and in the world above the feminine, continually is "led forth to his kingdom," and does not discover her own realm.

How, then, might we imagine an alternative ending? The Grimms' story tells us that we begin the journey toward individuation, like the servant girl of our tale, identified for the most part with and by the roles we play in our society. Our "feminine consciousness" is most often a consciousness merged with feminine gender persona. Stripped of that persona by outer and inner events, fearful and confused, we begin to discover a selfhood that is prior to and independent of our roles and our relationships with others. We may notice in ourselves qualities and capacities that we have learned to regard as "masculine," and we will discover these possibilities in our dreams as "animus figures," masculine players in the dramas of the soul. Unlike the servant girl, the contemporary woman may learn to regard these figures as aspects of her own soul's reality, the qualities they display as truly her own, for good or ill. Through such encounter and recognition, consciousness of self and other is clarified and enlarged, and the masculine figures we encounter in dreams and the men to whom we are drawn in the outer world will begin to change.

When a woman no longer dreams, for example, of the brilliant male scholar, it may be because she has recognized and integrated logos qualities which she has heretofore assumed to be masculine, not fully her own, but subject to masculine approval and authority. Her expression of logos abilities will then be neither tentative and fearful nor "animus possessed." Further encounters with masculine figures displaying other unrealized qualities may then challenge her, first to relationship, then to further integration and enactment of the potential they offer. Always these figures draw us deeper into psyche, toward an encounter with the Self.

And at last we may come face to face with a feminine source at the heart of the undiscovered territory of the soul. Unlike the servant girl of our story, if we are conscious of both dark and light potentials of the feminine Self, we will then be forced to recognize that its power, in a "plain" and limited form, is our own, no longer to be identified as masculine and therefore essentially "other," or alien to ourselves, no longer to be projected upon the men in our lives. When we then leave the forest of potential for action in the world, we will do so knowing and accepting that the responsibilities of choice and consequence cannot be surrendered to masculine others.

We may be challenged, therefore, to a deeper and more conscious integration of seeming opposites: autonomy and the requirements of relationship, initiative and receptivity, effective action in the private and in the public realms, personal expression and the nurture of others. Perhaps we will find a primary value in authenticity, a willingness to rely upon the guidance of the Self, and the courage to sacrifice old illusions of security.

Let us imagine, then, a furthering of our story:

S ome years passed happily for the king's son and his bride. Yet it was not long before small troubles appeared, and they grew larger with time. The king's son grew restless, for the old king lived on, and although he grew dim of vision and ever more feeble in action, he would not relinquish authority to his son. Indeed, he grew more oppressive as his powers waned and his fears increased. The king's son chafed at his restrictions, as did the king's subjects, but no one could challenge the leader they both loved and feared.

In his trouble, the king's son grew distant from his wife, forgetting at last that it was she who had freed him from enchantment in the forest of the Old Woman. Now he saw her as the cause of his present bondage, and he thought with increasing longing of the days when he had roamed his father's kingdom, free to enjoy the privileges of royal youth. Then a king to the south, perceiving the weakness and division in his neighbor's realm, threatened war. The king's son was freed, at last, into action, and he rode away at the head of his men, not without misgiving, but determined to do what he could in defense of the kingdom which might, after all, one day be his.

Now once again the girl who was the king's son's wife felt herself abandoned, and she saw that the eyes of the court and of the old king himself looked on her with open scorn, for to them she had never been more than a servant girl who had somehow caught a king's son for husband. Whispers against her grew into mutters, and it began to be said that the troubles in the kingdom must be the fault of this alien girl. Had she not, after all, come from the forest of the Old Woman? No doubt she herself was a sorceress, for how else could she have won for herself the son of a king? The girl withdrew and sat day after day alone in her room, and no one attended her save one old woman, the least of the household of the king. In her loneliness, the girl pondered her life, and sometimes she felt that injustice had followed her all of her days, and sometimes she thought that the king and the court must be right: that she herself harbored an evil that drew evil upon her and those that she loved.

She looked at the old woman who served her and thought that she saw evil there and was afraid, for she remembered the Old Woman in the wood and the power of enchantment she held. In all of the kingdom, only this old one came near to her, and was this not a proof of her own low nature? But remembering her time in the wood, she began to dream of the food and the rest she had had there in the trees, and it seemed not so different, after all, from the care the old servant provided. I have done nothing for her, the girl thought, or for myself, and still she comes to me without fail. The girl grew curious and began to question her attendant and to listen carefully to her replies. The old woman, it soon appeared, had stories to tell and more stories, and old songs to sing in her cracked old voice, and the more the girl listened, the wiser the old woman seemed, and the stronger she herself grew.

Now she remembered the ring, the plain gold ring she had taken away from the Old Woman's house. No one had ever worn it, for it did not fit the hand of the king's son, and she had not presumed to try it for herself. It was stored away in the treasury of the king, the forgotten emblem of the king's son's release from the forest. She thought she must find it, for she wanted to give something to the old servant, in gratitude for all her help and counsel. In all the king's household, the ring was the only thing she felt she might claim as hers to give, for she was the one who had won it away. She remembered her fears on that day and the love that had overcome them, but now there was no dove to advise her. Still, desire grew in her, and at last she went before the king.

When she stated her wish and her claim, fear made her voice small and her manner falsely sweet, and the king made no response. He looked at her sternly and thought to himself, what secret does she hide? He remembered the ring had magic of a sort and recalled the rumors that charged his son's wife with the power of sorcery. "That ring you may not have," he told the girl at last, "but I own many jewels much richer than the plain gold ring, and I will give you one for your adornment." So he thought to flatter her vanity and win her gratitude, for although he could not let it be known, he found himself in fear of her. But the girl would not be swayed, and said, "I wish only to receive again the plain gold ring."

Now the king's doubt and fear turned to anger. On that very day he had heard of his son's defeat in battle. The forces of the southern king had breached the borders of his realm, and suddenly it seemed clear to the king that this girl who stood before him, this strange girl with her strange requests, must surely be the cause of all the ills that had grown in his kingdom since she had come there. "My son is lost to me," he cried, "and you are no more the wife of the son of a king." The girl fell down before him, and the king cried out again, "If you would live on as his widow, begone at once, and let me never more behold you!"

The girl fled from the throne room, fled from the castle, blinded by grief, goaded by fear. On and on she ran until at last she fell exhausted to the ground and slept. She woke in the light of a full moon and found herself once again in the deep woods, in a clearing surrounded by the great trees she knew so well. Eyes shone upon her from the dark forest, but when the girl cried out, "Who is there?" no answer came. Again she called, "Come closer, I fear you not at all. If you would have my life, it is yours, for all that gave it value in the world is lost to me." Now a rustling grew in the margin of the clearing, and forms emerged, large and small, and the girl saw that all those who called the forest home drew near. Small figures scurried close and deer stepped daintily, regarding her with large calm eyes. A bear drew himself erect before her, grunting and swaying, and sinuous large cats bounded into view. In the midst of them all appeared a tall cloaked Woman, stern and regal in her bearing, and all the wild creatures drew back to give her place before the girl.

"My sisters," said she, "have served you well. Now, if you would live, and serve the life which has begun to grow within you, you must give your service to my cause." The girl agreed, and so she learned of the child to be born of her union with the prince. For a time and a time she labored then, performing with good grace the tasks the tall stern Woman put before her. Under her direction the girl baked and brewed and swept and cleaned, and learned new skills as well. beautiful weavings grew under her hands, and pots and jars for both storage and display, and the healing arts, with root and herb, became her own to use. Songs grew full and clear inside her, and she gave words and music to her longing and her fear, her anger and her love. Above all, she learned the ways of the deep woods, conforming herself to the seasons ruling there, discovering the time and the value of yes and of no, how forming gives way to dissolution, and life and death rule always side by side.

Her daughter was born and grew sturdy in the house of the tall Woman, playing beside her mother there and roaming ever more widely the deep corridors of the forest. Her mother wondered now and then what might be the cause the Woman had said she must serve, for it seemed to her that she and her daughter were the ones that were served by her life in the Woman's abode. And then one day, sent far from the house in search of particular herbs, the young mother sat to rest by a deep pool.

The pool lay at the base of a mighty rock and gathered its clear, pure waters from a spring that burst from an opening high in the rock face. Watercress grew in the calm margins of the pool, and the young mother thought to gather some to grace their supper. As she leaned out, she caught sight of her face mirrored there, and she marveled at the changed self she beheld. Sorrow and struggle and necessity had marked her, certainly, but the long calm hours of learning and reflection showed as well, and the love that flowed among the three, the Woman and herself and her own small daughter. Her face, she saw, had become the face of a woman, strong and serene, bearing the lines of both laughter and grief.

It came to her then that her time in the forest must end. She would return to the land she had fled that long while ago and see how she might live there with her daughter, for it seemed to her now that she had something to learn and something to teach among the people there. She thought of her lost love and of the battles that had taken him from her, and she felt again her grief and her fear. Who might rule now in the land, she wondered, and how might she be received there, changed as she was? Yet she must go.

She returned to the house of the Woman, not forgetting the herbs for which she had come nor the watercress, gift of the forest pool. The tall Woman met her on the path, and together they walked and talked, and planned for the journey she must take. The day came, and she was well prepared, and she and her daughter went forth from the forest to find where the path might lead. She went assured that the forest and the Woman who lived in its heart would abide, and that she would find her way to them whenever they had need of her or she of them.

And so the story ends, and does not end, for we do not know yet how the woman and her daughter will fare in a changing world. Perhaps the king's son did not, after all, die in his war with the forces that challenged the old king's rule. Perhaps he and the kingdom, although altered by struggle and loss, survive to recognize and to welcome the changed woman, and they two may begin, meeting and parting and meeting again, to create together a new dance of life.

REFERENCES

Grimm, the Brothers. 1975. *Complete Grimm's Fairy Tales*. London: Routledge and Kegan Paul.

von Franz, M.-L. 1972. *The Feminine in Fairy Tales*. New York: Spring Publications.

———. 1980. *An Interpretation of Apuleius' Golden Ass*. Irving, Texas: Spring Publications.

Jung, C. G. 1954. The philosophical tree. *Collected Works* 13:251–349. Princeton, N.J.: Princeton University Press, 1967.

Neumann, Erich. 1959. The psychological stages of feminine development. Rebecca Johnson, trans. *Spring* (1959):63–67, Kraus reprint, 1975.

"Oisin's Mother"
Because I Would Not Give My Love to the Druid Named Dark

Claire Douglas

What I'm about to tell is a fairy tale that lies in the middle of a long family history. It concerns a maiden, a deer, some dogs, an evil druid, and a hero king. There are magic spells and shape shifts. The story is also about incest, victimization, and pain. These remain unhealed and unresolved in this telling, although a child is born who carries the tale, or problem, or dream a bit further. In Jungian terms, it's a story about projections and being caught by the opposites. In personal terms, it has much to say about childhood sexual abuse and its sequelae. The story takes place at the point where many of my patients start in therapy or where they have just remembered what they had spent a whole lifetime forgetting. They have been damaged by a too potent and too early experience of an invasive other and often seem incapable of relationship. The fairy tale concerns the shame and horror of what happened and the pain of reexperiencing victimization. The part that integrates the trauma and that most terrible negative animus—the inner rapist and relative—belongs to a later story, although he is dramatically present here.

   The fairy tale could be told from many points of view. I will concentrate on its clinical importance for women. I do this because many of my patients are women who have suffered physical or psychological sexual abuse and because so little has been written in Jungian literature from a woman's and survivor's perspective. This story helps image and clarify aspects of the problem by presenting it in archetypal form. Bettleheim writes that "in a fairy tale internal processes are externalized and become comprehensible as represented by the figures of the story and its events" (1977, p. 25). Children (and the child in us) use fairy tales both to universalize and to work out their own conflicts. I hope this fairy tale can be of use in understanding some of the experience and conflicts of this particular problem, and that it may also speak to those whose inner child suffers from a similar wound.

A Celtic fairy tale seldom stands alone. It is like one dream embedded in a series. Also, like a dream, its sense of time is circular, its space meanders; nothing goes straight to the point. What happens now is dependent on what came after as well as what comes before. Things shift with the very mists of the earth, happen on many levels at once, and often are a bit different from what they seem. In short, the Celtic tale (and soul), like the psyche, is at home in mythopoesis, that other, more holographic, way we think "which allows an object to be understood, not by a single and consistent definition, but by various and unrelated approaches. . . . What appears usually as subordinate may suddenly, under the influence of a narrower but concentrated attention, gain the weight of an independent entity. It may even absorb the whole of which it once was a part. . . . Connotations may differ from case to case" (Frankfort 1978, pp. 61–62). (There are many variations on this tale. My main source has been *Irish Fairy Tales* by James Stephens (1920, pp. 109–132).)

Oisin's Mother

O nce upon a time there was a beautiful girl of the Danann named Saeve. She lived the carefree life of a young fairy maiden until, one dread day, the Black Magician of the Men of God cast his eye on her "and, after that day, in whatever direction she looked" (Stephens 1920, p. 116) she saw his eye on her. Wherever she looked or went, he was there watching her. In all places and all times, she would try to escape, but he would find her and there he'd be gazing on her again. It was a gaze that made her feel very strange and it frightened her to the core of her being. But he was the great Black Druid and she was just a young relative. She had no words to clothe these odd feelings and, besides, had no one to talk to about him, his dark greatness and her horror. So Saeve's terror grew and grew until, at last, as he approached her ever closer, she could stand it no longer. Her eyes grew as large and fearful as a deer's, and she fled in panic: a nimble and beautiful fawn.

One evening, "a golden-shafted, tender-coloured eve" (ibid., p. 111), it happened that Fionn, the white, the chief of the Fianna-Finn and a king of Ireland, was returning from the hunt, when Saeve, as a fawn, darted out in front of him. Fionn was with his two favorite hounds, Bran and Sceolan. They were the canine offspring, it seems, of another woman who had been shape-shifted into animal form. The dogs at once recognized that the fawn, like them, was other than she appeared. She led them away, they and Fionn pursued, until the four were in a safe place. There the fawn rested, frolicked with the dogs, and allowed Fionn to befriend her and lead her home. That night, the king's door opened and Saeve appeared as a young maiden again. She was "shy as a flower, beautifully timid as a fawn" (ibid., p. 115). She told Fionn her story and added that she had wandered in deer form "because I would not give my love to the Druid of the Fairy Folk. . .named Dark" (Rolleston 1911, p. 267). After three years of this wandering, she had learned from one of the druid's slaves that she would find safety in Fionn's castle. Only there would she be free of the terror of the Dark Man. Fionn at once declared his undying love for her and offered her his protection and his hand in marriage.

They lived for some time completely enraptured with each other and oblivious to the rest of the world. It was the very survival of Ireland that finally bestirred Fionn from her side. He departed to fight off the invaders who were harrassing Ireland's shore. He fought bravely and well against the enemies of Ireland, defeated them, and returned to his wife as quickly as he could. Alas, he found his castle in uproar and Saeve gone.

What had happened was this. Saeve had been looking down from the castle walls, when, only a day or so after his departure, she thought she saw him returning. He was in full battle dress and his hounds, Bran and Sceolan, were with him, or so it seemed. Against the entreaties of the servants and guards, she raced down to meet her love and to tell him the news that she was with child. She was just about to throw herself in his arms when she realized in horror that it was not Fionn, her love, but the Black Magician disguised as Fionn! The druid tapped her with his hazel rod and, on the spot, she turned again into a shivering deer. She raced for the castle's gate, for home. Three times Saeve broke away, three times the Dark Druid's hounds of hell caught up with her, seized her by the throat, and dragged her back to him. The soldiers dashed out to save her, but as they reached the captive, she, the hounds, and the Black Magician vanished. There was nothing left but a heavy mist, the sound of beating feet, the baying of hounds, and then a silent and empty plain.

The end of the story is that Fionn hunted the world for Saeve for seven long years. He searched the length and breadth of Ireland, following deer tracks wherever he found them and wherever they would lead him. Just as he was about to give up, his wise old hounds suddenly broke away from him and raced toward a hill. Here, they formed a circle and battled off many yelping dogs. Fionn caught up with them and saw, in the middle of the ring they'd made, a naked little boy. " 'We have caught something on this hunt. We must bring the treasure home,' " said Fionn (Stephens 1920, p. 128). As the boy and he looked at each other, the boy's noble trust and fearlessness melted Fionn's heart. Fionn called him Oisin, the little fawn, for he had realized that the boy had Saeve's eyes and that he was their son.

Fionn took his son home. As Oisin learned to talk, he told Fionn that he had been all alone for as long as he could remember except for a deer who loved him. She fed him on berries and herbs and warmed him and protected him as best she could. But all too often a dark, stern man visited her. "Sometimes he talked gently and softly and coaxingly, but at times again he would shout loudly and in a harsh, angry voice. But whatever way he talked the deer would draw away from him in dread, and he always left her at last furiously" (ibid., p. 131). Finally, one day, the Black Druid touched the deer again with his hazel rod and, under a spell, she was forced to follow him. She looked back at Oisin and cried piteously and longingly as she was led away, but, try as he might, he could not follow her. Then came the attacking dogs, a different world from hers, Fionn's hounds defending him, and here he was. Oisin grew up to be a great fighter and an even greater poet. He sang the songs of the old days and recounted the stories of the Shi (Fairy), but of his mother nothing more was known from that day to this.

I will recapitulate the bare bones of this tale. A maiden flees the embraces of her relative, a dark and powerful man, by turning herself into a fawn. A white and powerful man and his two half-human dogs rescue her. She regains human form and marries the man of light. She lives for a time enraptured by him. The dark man recaptures her by appearing in the shape of the light man. She is turned back into a deer, bears a human son to the white man, but vanishes with the dark one. The son and father are reunited; the son becomes a poet and a warrior.

One fruitful way of understanding a fairy tale or a dream is to take each character and element and examine it from every angle. Exploring the objective, subjective, archetypal, and personal meanings behind each figure is part of the weaving that needs to be done. Here, I'll be concerned with some of the archetypal and psychological meanings attached to each of the major threads of the tale. These are the black and white split animus figures of the druid and Fionn; the animal motifs – dog, fawn, and deer; the character of Saeve, the maiden; the psychological sequelae of incest and victimization as they are exemplified in this fairy tale, and, finally, the family history of the problem and its resolution when a descendant brings about her own liberation and healing.

Druids were the Celt's priests, judges, seers, healers, scientists, magicians, and poets. They were an exclusive and very powerful group. They could be male or female but had to be of noble birth. Druids underwent very long and rigorous training; twenty years is the number most often given. They married consanguineously and within their group. They always dressed in white robes and are identifiable by these robes (Jobes 1962, Cavendish 1970, Norton-Taylor 1974, Piggott 1987).

The particular druid of this story, however, dresses in black and is named Dark. This is odd. He is a black, not a white druid and, besides, inhabits fairy land: a land both below and beyond the normal. It was often thought to be underground or undersea. Lady Wilde (1899) in her collection of Celtic lore, writes of this, and that the Tuatha-de-Dananns, the fairies, were considered to be angels who had been cast out from heaven. She describes the Celtic belief that they were an ancient race of fallen angels who excelled in necromancy, magic, music, poetry, architecture, and horse breeding (see also Kennedy 1866 and Evans-Wentz 1966). Fairies and druids, it would seem therefore, have similar talents: one natural, the other after long training. A druid of the fairies thus would be a noble among the fallen angels and a doubly potent magician.

The Black Druid, from what we have learned so far, seems to have a lot in common with Satan, the leader of the fallen angels in the Bible. Like Milton's Satan, he has a proud will and, like him, is filled with concupiscence. His sexuality is focused upon an apparently incestuous relationship. Sandra Gilbert and Susan Gubar (1980) write about Milton's Satan's dark, Promethean demonism as deeply misogynist yet, at the same time, as exerting a peculiarly hypnotic attraction for women. They describe him as a type of Byronic hero who revels in a bruising yet earthy masculinity. The Black Magician of the Men of God is barely sketched in the fairy tale, his character left to the plot and to the mythopoetic imagination, yet he shares Milton's fallen angel's unredeemed chthonicism and sensual power. This druid named Dark may be seen as the Terrible Mother's phallic and Dionysian aspect in its most malevolent form. He is the self-indulgent breaker of all rules and, like Hades, is the rapist who cruelly abducts the maiden. He is the negative representative of the chthonic masculine: Satan, Hades, Dionysus, Bly's (1986) Wild Man, at their most reprehensible. He wounds, attacks, and spellbinds poor Saeve.

An intense experience of this type of potent yet assaultive masculinity in the form of a trusted relative, the Dark Druid, is especially damaging and confusing to a young child. The child is brought up to trust and respect her relative but he turns out to be treacherous. There's often a tremendous need to keep the druid loveable, especially if he's the only one who gives the child attention or affection. The child needs to idealize the object, so blames herself for what happened to her. It's the only way for the child to make sense of her universe. How could the adult and this adult's actions be anything but the normal way of the world, what druids do? Yet she feels it's all wrong for her, and so the child becomes unsure of the world and its meanings. She also becomes as guilty and shamefilled as if she committed the crime. What she has experienced is so vile (the touch of the druid named Dark) that what she longs for becomes impossibly pure (Fionn, in all his one-sided perfection). As with torture victims, there might have been some body-stirring, some sexual response mixed with Saeve's terror and pain that makes it far, far worse. It's sometimes not just the sex but the bizarreness of it that makes the flesh crawl and scrambles development; dark powers get stirred up before the ego is secure. One result can be panic and flight: life as a fawn replaces growing up. And sometimes worst of all, there's no safety anywhere. There's no safe place to hide from the druid, "wherever she went he was there," even in one's room, even in sleep. Forgetting, then, becomes a protection, sometimes a life-saving one, as does icing out, splitting off, not being there (as invisible as a fawn). Instead of the relationship she longs for, the child experiences a terrifying sense of aloneness (alone as a deer in the woods). What she has experienced also involves her in a dark forest of secrets in which betrayal, even by her own instincts, lurks everywhere. Besides that, society, her family, and she herself all either don't want to hear about such a monstrosity or need to deny it (it happened to a deer, not to Saeve).

The wound in this fairy tale, as in actual incest, at first seems too deep to transform. The process begins, though, through this very separation and division with the opposites appearing one-sidedly differentiated: the blackest of villains versus the noblest of heroes. In treating incest or victims of child abuse, I think the character of the abuser first needs to be acknowledged in all his charged malevolence, the damage he has caused witnessed fully. However, if this fairy tale were a dream, I'd take it as a sign that now something was about to move. The clarity of the villain's very negativity holds the hope for future internal transformation and integration. Since all characters have their other side, and what is new in the psyche often appears first in its most terrible form, I'd wonder what the other side of the internal druid might be and if he, too, might bring something positive and healing if he could be dealt with within Saeve's own psyche. I cannot think of a more difficult task for a woman who suffered attack from him as a child.

In "The Phenomenology of the Spirit in Fairy Tales," Jung writes of a similar evil magician as a "sinister father-imago of subterrene nature" (1948, par. 433). The druid is, in Neumann's (1970) terms, a representative and an ally of the Terrible Mother who pulls the hero away from consciousness and backward toward chaos and disorder. Jung writes:

> This represents a principle which, by reason of its symbolism, betrays affinity with evil, though it is by no means certain that it expresses nothing but evil. Everything points rather to the fact that evil, or its familiar symbolism, belongs to the family of figures which describe the dark, nocturnal, lower, chthonic element . . . . He [the wicked magician] has remained in the realm of the dark mother, caught by the wolfish greed of the unconscious which is unwilling to let anything escape from its magic circle. (1948, par. 425)

What else do we know of the Dark Druid? As in most fairy tales, he is seen from the outside and is one-sided (Tatar 1987). He carries the shadow masculine and is the evil element of the story (von Franz 1980). He is also the shadow part of Saeve. The Dark Druid lusts for a relative; he is full of anger, selfish desire, and dark powers. He has a powerful (hazel) rod. He can take on the shape of another man, but his magic is not infinite. He argues with, pleads with, harangues, terrifies, and pursues Saeve before he seizes her. After bewitching her, he, for a time, falls under certain restrictions and only has recourse to words and emotion. It is his slave (psychologically an inferior or repressed part of the druid) who gives Saeve the information she needs for her temporary escape. The druid's chthonicism, his similarities to Satan and Hades, and his leading Saeve back to the underworld accompanied by the baying of hounds, all make him a sinister symbol of death. We don't know what happens to the Black Magician after he captures Saeve and leads her out of the story, again a prisoner of the power of darkness. His story off-stage is incomplete.

Fionn, on the other hand, appears in many other stories, legends, and fairy tales. He was a hero and lived a heroic life. His birth was the result of his mother's rape by another powerful druid. Fionn had to hide from her husband, the chief of an opposing clan, and was reared by others in secret. Two druid women brought him up: one a famous runner and athlete, the other a sage. He had a magic, future-revealing thumb because, at the start of his adventures, he had tasted a druid's salmon, the salmon of knowledge. He was a brave warrior, had many adventures, and became chief or high king of Ireland. He saw his grandson, Oisin's son Oscar, die in battle, but nothing is told about Fionn's own death. He, like the Black Druid, simply exits, little changed by his adventures.

Fionn's name means whiteness or fairness. He is also known as the Fair One and was renowned for his valor, gentleness, and generosity. He loved his animals, especially his dogs, and they returned his love. He also spent much time hunting animals and killing deer. In illustrations, he is shown wearing deerskin robes. Fionn gained the salmon's uncanny knowledge, so he, too, has some relationship to the earthy, animal, instinctive, and chthonic realms, although, in this story, he is presented as one-sidely noble and pure. He trusted his animals about Saeve, the fawn, and did not harm her. In her human form, he fell in love with her at first sight and is as passionate as the Black Druid.

"She is the Sky-woman of the Dawn," he said. "She is the light on the foam. She is white and odorous as an apple-blossom. She smells of spice and honey. She is my beloved beyond the women of the world. She shall never be taken from me."

And the thought was delight and anguish to him: delight because of the sweet prospect, anguish because it was not yet realized. (Stephens 1920, p. 115)

Fionn is deeply moved by Saeve. Something in her calls out the tender hero in him who wants to rescue, protect, and defend her (maybe also in unconscious response to the rape of his mother that resulted in his own birth). He married Saeve the first day he met her and, like the druid, tried to envelop her in an illusory magic circle. Fionn and Saeve made a magic circle in which the two feasted on nothing but their love. It is a fairy tale *folie à deux*, a sort of love trance, that is as full of illusion and flight as Saeve's other lives. If I were writing about this fairy tale from a man's standpoint, I'd stress Fionn's anima infatuation. Von Franz writes in *The Feminine in Fairy Tales* that, "feminine figures in fairy tales are neither the pattern of the anima nor of the real woman, but of both, because sometimes it is one, and sometimes another . . . . A good approach is to interpret the tale both ways" to see which focus yields the most material (1976, p. 3). Saeve carries Fionn's anima projection for him, she may even hide herself in this projection by hiding in their love within the castle. It is an interesting question whether, through his own psychology, Fionn forced her to carry and live out his anima or whether it is one more needed disguise for Saeve, or both. In any case, their relationship, if one can call an infatuation a relationship, cannot and does not last. As soon as Fionn returns to normal life, he loses her for good. His effort to rescue her fails. It is almost as if Saeve were making a panicky flight into health. The long, patient working out of their relationship never happens. Things take place too quickly and too one-sidedly for the lovers once they find each other.

According to Neumann's (1970) schema of development, the hero gains in consciousness nonetheless. Fionn, the hero, does this by having once rescued the captive (anima) and then again and more solidly, after a long and patient search, through gaining the treasure, his child (a symbol of the Self). The Black Druid and Fionn, however, never meet and never fight it out. Neither loses his power, neither has congress with the other; they remain in static opposition. (Fionn's chthonic thumb of knowledge is never put to use in a search for either the druid or Saeve. It isn't even mentioned in any of the versions of this fairy tale. Its prominence in some other tales and its absence here make me conjecture that his anima infatuation dulled his instincts and his intuition.)

Saeve, however, deals with both the white hero and the black magician, although she, too, keeps them apart. She moves from one extreme to the other. She dreads and hates the negative, evil druid while idealizing her white king, yet she mistook the sinister one for the idealized one as soon as Fionn left their magic circle. She ends up as a deer and in thrall to the negative, her druid named Dark. This ricocheting from one opposite to the other is a key element in the fairy tale and in the psychology of incest victims. It depicts a classic case of impaired object-relations. Someone is either all light or all dark; the two cannot be allowed to intermingle. This type of impaired object-relations makes forming and maintaining relationships particularly hazardous for a woman. The split can involve her in physical sexuality that is cut off from feeling, or vice versa. She can present a history of many brief and unsatisfactory affairs with the druid turning into Fionn or Fionn into the druid just when the woman thinks she has them straight. It can also involve a woman in intensely negative feelings toward men and/or in overvaluing them. There is often a repeated search for Fionn, a hero, protector, and savior, who inevitably is scanned for the slightest defect, and, just as inevitably, this trusted hero, showing a failing or two, abruptly changes into the all-evil druid. Re-victimization becomes inevitable and along with it feelings of lack of power over her own life. The hero, so impossibly pure, can seem unreachable; besides this, the victim can feel too guilty to merit him. She can become, instead, drawn to abusing, battering, or sadistic men (often initially misperceived as savior heroes) and feel she deserves this abuse. (See Herman and Hirschman (1977), Butler (1978), Renvoize (1982), Forward and Buck (1984), Russell (1986), for these and further typical psychological effects of incest.)

The animal side of nature is also split. In the fairy tale I have been discussing, the animals are Fionn's two dogs, Bran and Sceolan, and their ghostly doubles, the hounds of the Dark Druid; the fawn Saeve turned herself into to escape the druid, and the deer into which he turned her in order to recapture her again. Jung writes of animals in fairy tales as portraying functions and contents of an archetype in extra-human form (1948, par. 419). He writes that animals represent the archetype at the instinctive level and portray aspects that are both above and below human consciousness. He emphasizes the importance of understanding the characteristics of the particular animals in the fairy tale or dream.

The relevant characteristics of the animals in this story are complex and many-sided. In Celtic lore, dogs are associated with healing springs. They accompany hunters, warriors, and healers. Bran and Sceolan were both females. Bran is described by Lady Wilde as "a ferocious, small-eared, white-breasted, sleek-haunched hound; having the eyes of a dragon, the claws of a wolf, the vigor of a lion, and the venom of a serpent" (1899, p. 148). She was the wisest and fleetest of dogs, could show sorrow, cried real tears, and had a foreknowledge of evil. Yet, in this story, just as Fionn makes no use of the knowledge in his thumb, Bran does not warn him of impending evil. (Bran and Sceolan remind me of Xanthus and Balius in the Iliad – the half-human horses of Achilles at the siege of Troy, who also foretold the future and could cry human tears.) Bran and Sceolan, as previously stated, were half-human because their mother was bewitched into dog form at the time of their conception and birth. Fionn loved Bran, his unconscious animal feminine, the best of all his hounds. Fionn is supposed to have cried twice – once when Bran died and the other time when Fionn's own grandson, Oscar, was killed.

Dogs' relationship to hunters and healers is found cross-culturally. (Jobes (1962), Cooper (1978), and Cirlot (1982), are my chief sources for amplification on animal symbology.) Dogs' sense of smell is acute and they are excellent trackers. They pick up information differently from humans, so balance and complement our ways of knowing. Dogs are also supposed to guard the boundaries between this world and the next. They are supposed to see as well at night as in the day so make good guides to the underworld. In this aspect, they serve as psychopomps attending the dead and are associated with Chiron, Hades, Hecate, and Anubis. A dog also guided the goddess, Isis, in her search for Osiris, and dogs are often associated with other great goddesses such as Ishtar and Gula. As hunters, dogs are sacred to the maiden goddesses, Diana and Artemis, who are both virgin goddesses and yet have orgiastic celebrations. As healers they are associated with Hermes and Aesculapius. In the Bible and in folktale, they heal through licking the sores of the afflicted. In shamanism they are considered messengers of the forest spirits. Hecate's presence is signified by the distant howling of her hounds. She and her dogs represent the sinister dark side of the moon (at least to those with solar consciousness). Demon dogs are associated with Hecate and with Yama, the Hindu god of death. Black dogs, like the little poodle in Goethe's *Faust*, and generally in folklore, are, or are connected with, the devil. As such, they can represent dangerous and demonic powers and can be made use of in sorcery.

The dogs in this fairy tale are clearly double; on one side, faithful to the hero, Fionn, they are gentle to the heroine and rescue the son; on the other, they carry out the demonic and cruel commands of the villainous druid, treat the heroine brutally, and attack the boy. In Barbara Hannah's (1954) lectures on the psychological meaning of the cat, dog and horse, she notes the remarkably dual attributes of dogs. Dogs in dreams, Hannah says, are positive and helpful when a person honors the instincts, but show up in angry and demonic form when the instincts are repressed. She finds that dogs are the animal most representative of instinctual life and appear when the instinct is closest to consciousness; with this often comes some acknowledgment of one's own more shadowy dog qualities, such as the dog's promiscuous sexuality, its rage, and its trickster qualities.

While a dog's most acute sense is his sense of smell, a fawn has no smell. It is silent and odorless. It has protective coloring that blends with the sunlight and shadows on the grass in which it hides. It avoids attack through its stillness. It defends itself through not appearing to be there at all, through an optical illusion vanishing act. A fawn has an anima-like beauty, delicacy, wildness, shyness, and grace. Its sensitivity causes it to quiver and cringe. As a verb, to fawn means to curry favor or affection through fearful or subservient insincerity. Jobes (1962) relates this to the way a fawn will quiveringly lick the hand of someone who feeds it. Fawns seldom appear in other guises, although in Dionysian mysteries, they are suckled by the maenads one minute and torn apart the next. A faun is not a real fawn, but since dreams and fairy tales pun, it may hold a shadow aspect of the meaning. A faun is a sensual, rural demigod who is a man above the waist and a randy goat beneath (Saeve's inner druid).

The symbolism of the deer is as complex and many-sided as that of the dog. Overtly, they represent gentle beauty and otherworldliness. Deer are elegant, sure-footed, and graceful. A female deer is equated with the supposedly wifely virtue of docile, faithful affection, but in Chinese Buddhism this quality is seen in a different way and deer are considered one of the three "senseless creatures" and denote love-sickness. The deer, like the horse, has an instantaneous panic reaction to danger: both spook easily and flee at the slightest alarm. Yet the fleeing deer was taken by the Jews as representing victory in defeat for it was seen as the soul caught by death or by God the hunter. A deer at a well symbolizes a soul thirsting for God or longing for rebirth into a better land. Jung writes that the deer sometimes signifies the Self as lapis (1955–1956, par. 188 and 188n). In Celtic mythology, they were the fairies' cattle and supernatural messengers, and so chasing a deer in a fairy tale often means that the protagonist has entered a magical situation.

Deer have another and more potent side. In many cultures, shamans wear deer skin and antlers to ally themselves with this power. Deer, along with dogs, are sacred to Artemis, Diana, and Hermes and are allied with Athene and Aphrodite. While a dog can represent overt masculine desire, a white deer signifies hidden female desire. In this aspect, it is secretly allied with snakes, having the ability to draw snakes out of their dens and into the open. A shadow aspect of the gentle deer is its fury; it is noted both for its sexual fury and for its capacity to suddenly turn on, lash out at, and try to trample its tamer. The shy, gentle side of the deer is its most obvious aspect in this tale, but these darker meanings reverberate in projection onto the druid.

All the animals in this fairy tale are female. They provide a missing feminine element, the missing fourth to complete the quaternity. The ethereal heroine, Saeve, plus the instinctive animal feminine of the deer and dogs, join with the masculine hero and villain to make up the quaternity in the fairy tale. That the feminine fourth has to appear in animal, not human, form in the story seems a problem of our culture. Even the Celts, who were so much more accepting of all aspects of the feminine, were long christianized at the time of the telling of this fairy tale and so the tale has absorbed some of the splitness that Christianity encouraged. Our culture has denied the instinctual and chthonic to women even more than it has to men. Thus the dark feminine, the earthy, sensual, vigorously active "yang-femininity" (from Haddon 1987) remains in the unconscious. It is repressed or only present as shadow stuff. A survivor of child abuse claims the dark power of the feminine with perilous difficulty. Often there seems to be no coherent central personality able, yet, to claim anything; instead, there may be both fusion and schizoidal splitting. Boundaries have become blurred, because the child's body's boundaries were invaded before she had an integrated body image; her instincts might just as easily be her own, the druid's, Fionn's, or an animal's; blurred like this, instincts become dangerous and have to be split off.

Some abused women identify with the split-off shadow part and live out the demon, chthonic side alone. For the Saeve type, though, aggressive energies feel eaten up, they seem unembodied as if they live in a mist, in fairyland, not on the earth ("there was nothing left but the sound of beating feet, the baying of hounds, and then a silent and empty plain"). Assimilation of the shadow, not identification with it, grounds a person. But this shadow often feels so huge and brutal that it may be unassimilable or have to wait for years. And then there is the rage turned inward, the self-hate and villification. In order to shield herself from this, the survivor splits off both the internal rapist and the animal feminine; they operate unconsciously or in deeply separated compartments.

The final character in the tale is the central one, Saeve. She is an example of the archetypal Kore, the maiden part of the maiden–mother–Crone (or Hecate) aspects of the feminine. Yet Saeve had no mother that we know of and only the animal part of her bears and mothers a child. The Crone is most markedly absent. A Kore alone is thus incomplete and fragmentary. She lacks the (m)other who "extends feminine consciousness both upward and downwards" (1951, par. 316). She is the incomplete anima and incomplete "supraordinate personality" (ibid., par. 313) to which our culture endeavors to restrict the feminine. Saeve has much in common with Persephone and Ariadne, two other Kore figures. Like Persephone, she is an innocent maiden abducted and raped by an underworld power: Hades and the druid named Dark. Persephone descends to the underworld, though, in a true *nekyia*. She keeps her human form, marries her dark lord, and reigns as a powerful queen of the underworld. Persephone accepts the constraints and prohibitions of this realm and emerges, gloriously transformed and, in the Eleusinian mysteries, bears a child. She is ecstatically reunited with her mother and with the earth she loves. Poor Saeve had no such grounding from a caring mother and nothing is known of her in the Black Druid's realm, although she, too, births a male child. She did not marry the druid; her child was the child of Fionn, the white. Hades separated Persephone from symbiosis with her mother; this very separation led to her development as a person. Saeve lived an airy, unmothered life in fairyland; the Black Druid tore Saeve from no protective earthly mother. Saeve, ungrounded, fended for herself with what she had at hand: disguise, flight, and illusion in place of development.

Saeve shares with the Kore, Ariadne, the problem of opposing masculine images (or, psychologically, a split animus). Ariadne's were her half-brother, the labyrinthine bull, and Theseus, the shining warrior hero. She betrayed the dark one into the light one's power. Theseus engaged with and killed the minotaur, but also lost Ariadne, possibly through desertion. He and Fionn are conscious heroes. They both have developed sturdy, aggressive egos; they are at ease with their authority, are fighters capable of autonomous action, and both establish order in their realms. Yet both, in separating themselves from the matriarchy, involve themselves with a series of anima-like women. They have no meaningful relationship with women, often leaving, abandoning, or losing the feminine side of themselves. (Fionn's closest adult relationship to the feminine was to his dog, Bran.) In contrast to Fionn and Theseus, Ariadne reunites with her opposite, the chthonic masculine named Dark. She finds him, not as the bull, but transformed into Dionysus, and gives her love to him in this powerfully ecstatic form. Saeve flees the bull-power of the Dark Druid, cleaves to Fionn, the warrior hero, but, like Ariadne, loses him. Saeve's two masculine powers (or her split animus) never engage and she returns to the druid back in deer disguise, seemingly without any transformation.

Each of the three Kores — Saeve, Persephone and Ariadne — is raped, sacrificed, or abandoned. Persephone and Ariadne mature; their personalities become wiser and deeper. Each also takes on some of the aspects of both her light and her dark animi. Saeve remains the Kore, the sacrificial victim, and in disguise. This is the tragedy, often, for women whose experience of the outer masculine has been too violent and whose very souls seem to have been torn from them through early abuse. When a child has frightening or traumatic initial confrontations with the dark and sexual, "bull" masculine, this violent shadow often overlays later experience and interferes with a woman's relationship to inner and outer masculine figures. The inner masculine hero then, unmixed with his chthonic brother, becomes icily rational or heady, drives her to unmercifully heroic activity, and is murderously judgmental of the dark, the sensual, and unmaidenly feminine inside her. On the one side, the druid animus brutalizes the inner child-maiden and the deer, while, on the other, the virtuously judgmental animus punishes her for the very brutalization she experienced. All of this is terribly confusing to the child soul who eventually shows up in the consulting room and to the adult survivor there who wants to kill her inner child because she can't stand its pain. Both of them are parts of my patients, as are all the other jigsaw pieces, the part-personalities (Saeve, the deer, the fawn, the dogs, the hero, the villain, and Oisin, too, that small child).

An incest survivor confronting all the split-off parts of herself dreamed:

> My name is Iphigeneia* and I'm contemplating death and alternatives to suicide. Someone says it's a family curse. Someone else gives me some paper and I'm writing poem after poem. Z [her abuser] both wants sex and has a knife to cut my clitoris off 'cause I'm a whore. I yell "No! No way!" Someone is furious, says I wasn't condemned to death, I chose it. My mother's speaking poison: way she says things don't exist. That's why this second mother takes my mind to some sacred island for a while. I say it's all the same; someone says it isn't. I feel angry & hostile & rebellious & full of tears & sorrow. I feel torn apart by all these voices. Who to listen to? Who to believe?

A woman who is trying to reintegrate all these split-off parts of herself can often feel that she is going crazy. (Who else would understand that she really *did* turn into a deer?) She also may feel like killing herself, but it is only part of herself, whether victim, rapist, or the part who remembers the pain. However, I feel one of the biggest struggles an incest survivor has is wanting to live a human life, feeling she has a right to live rather than hiding in disguise or following the Dark Druid into death. The degree of effect seems independent of the severity of the abuse. But the effect is far more traumatic when the child/maiden is like Saeve and lacks mothering, lacks protection and comfort, lacks any

---

*When I was researching animal symbolism for this paper, I found out that in one version of a classical myth, Iphigeneia turned into a deer when her father, Agamemnon, was about to sacrifice her. Graves adds that the myth of the sacrifice cloaked a pattern of child sacrifice and "the mythographers' anxiety to conceal certain barbarous traditions" (1960, p. 78).

sense of power. This is a Kore without access to the mother and the Crone.

The third side of the Kore – the dark, underworld, Hecate side – is absent in Saeve's character. Her rage is the element most lacking in the story, unless, perhaps, the rage was turned inward and against herself when the Dark Druid took her over completely at the end. Other than that, it was all projected onto him. What is also missing is her own darkly potent female Lilith energy (Koltuv 1986). She lacks a yang-femininity that assertively stands up for itself and pleases itself rather than pleasing others. The Kore, Ariadne, was once Hagne the Queen of the Underworld and a powerful and orgiastic triple goddess (Kerenyi 1978 and Graves 1951). She is like the other dispossessed or abandoned goddesses that exist in all cultures and in all other psyches (such as Ereshkegal, Lilith, the Black Queen of Sheba, Pele who became a volcano, and the Yoruba goddess, Oya, who became the angry whirlwind). They were often either turned from central goddess figures into victims or were cast aside as archaic and negative representations of the terrible mother (like Kali or the Medusa, Athena's dark side). Saeve, though, is in a Celtic fairy tale, and Celtic goddesses kept their powerful trinity. The triple Morrigan, for example, holds all three sides of the feminine. There is a long lineage of Celtic war goddesses and Celtic women rulers, queens, generals, warriors, and druids who exulted in all aspects of themselves including rage. The Celtic culture welcomed huge waves of affect yet developed ways to tame them (Perera 1986) and include them in a woman's power. The only link Saeve has to any of this is the baying of the demon hounds: echoes of the underworld goddess that, in her story, are given to the druid named Dark whom she won't marry. She can't marry, merge, or war with the chthonic masculine because he assaulted her too early, before she could develop any sense of her own being or the right to her own destiny, and because she had lost access to her power. She lacks the human mother side and all of her third, Hecate, side. Because of this lack, it would not, as with the other Celtic women, have been a war or marriage between equals.

No wonder Saeve needs disguise or has to split off into different forms or part personalities, keeping one realm separate from the other. It is far safer for a terrified and traumatized woman to hide in invisibility like a fawn, or in the guise of a gentle deer, or yet again take on the disguise of a man's anima, "shy as a flower, beautifully timid as a fawn," than to risk facing all of who she is.

She has to start so far back and it involves reexperiencing so much pain. Besides that, she often has not only to recover an intact child self, iced away before or at the time of the trauma, and help it grow, but she has to gather together all the split-off parts of her psyche, including the seemingly inadmissible inner traumatizer.

One of the reasons a woman like Saeve has such trouble integrating this dark brother is that sexuality is so loaded for her. A woman facing this task dreamed that her sexual DNA had been so scrambled that it didn't code right. It never formed the same twisting helix twice or only did by chance. It was her task to go right back to that level to start unscrambling it. One of her problems in outer life was that this scramble, which felt so perilous to her, fascinated some men. It lent a deerlike, quivering uncertainty and innocence to a body that, unconsciously, also knew too much. Each time she made love it was, if it worked, a great wonder to her, but an arbitrary and unreliable one, that could also turn on her and suddenly become faunlike or even vicious. In outer life, it was far safer for her to slip into some man's anima (like Ariadne's mother, Pasiphae, did into the cow that Daedalus fashioned for her) and experience sexuality this way rather than to try to experience and unscramble her own.

Our culture holds many rewards for a woman who lives out a man's anima projection for him, so this is a problem many less traumatized women face, too. The culture approves the anima/maiden manifestation of the feminine but remains dubious about the other. Ariadne and Persephone, like Saeve, therefore get reduced to charming and helpless victims. Their original divine form, their ruling in the underworld, and their connection with the mother and the demonic feminine have tended to be overlooked. This now is changing. The Kore is starting to be seen in her multiplicity as a triune goddess. Women, especially, struggle with the new realization that each aspect is necessary for women's individuation.

Saeve had good animal instincts as a deer and made a careful and protective mother for her son. She left him with the knowledge that she loved him deeply. Yet she also left him for good when he was six or seven. At this age he would be emerging from uroboric containment and would need both his father and a greater consciousness than Saeve, the deer, could give him. She made a good enough mother for him until then, so Oisin was able to integrate the creative, poetic side of his mother and the heroic attributes of his father. Oisin must have been affected, though, by the "harsh angry voice" and dark druid moods that visited his mother. A mother's sadistic animus belaboring the frightened deer within mixes sulphurously with her tears. A child could not help but be affected by this dark aspect of his mother. Oisin, as we will see later, faced the same archetypal problem of the opposites in a slightly more integrated form.

The Kore lacking her other aspects becomes Saeve, the victim. She is helpless, vulnerable, powerless, and isolated. Her only defenses are flight and disguise. She hides, but does not escape, ricocheting from anguished victimization to a cloud-cuckoo land of rapture and idealization back into the devil's arms. Arthur Miller (1987) in his autobiography struggles to understand what happened between him and his wife, Marilyn Monroe. It is a most harrowing modern example of the archetypal situation of this fairy tale, with Miller cast into the role of the hero, Fionn, who becomes the villain, Dark. As hero, the role with which he identified, Miller's greatest desire was to save Monroe. She idealized him as spirit and intellect, as a safe, rational, and pure hero whose realm was cerebral and moral. In the book, Miller captures the futility of his efforts to carry this sort of animus projection and the heartbreaking pathos of the anima-like victim he could not save—Saeve, who lay behind Monroe's public image. He writes that "with all her radiance she was surrounded by a darkness that perplexed me" (1987, p. 307) and that she had a "seemingly endless anguish" (ibid., p. 429). He describes her brutalized and destroyed youth, perceiving that underneath all her humor and sophistication there lurked "an abused little girl. . .desperate for reassurance" (ibid., p. 448). This need for reassurance was coupled with a capacity for disguise that led her to master any image a man or a camera required. But when the reassurance stopped or when the disguise failed her, Monroe was at the mercy of an inner demon who turned her viciously against herself. Miller described their romance as starting with her complete idealization of him and his own acceptance of this idealization, with him fancying himself as her hero and savior. Their marriage failed when they both realized he couldn't maintain this role and when they left their magic circle in which, like Fionn and Saeve, they had been completely enraptured with each other and oblivious to the rest of the world. Instead of allowing him to become a normal man, Miller abruptly turned into, or Monroe turned him into, the blackest of villains. She believed he could save her, he jumped at the chance, and she hated him when he could not. The elements that link Monroe to Saeve continue in Miller's sad and searching words:

> Beneath all her insouciance and wit, death was her companion everywhere and at all times, and it may be that its unacknowledged presence was what lent her poignancy, dancing at the edge of oblivion as she was. (Ibid., p. 242)

> Marilyn lived in the belief that she was precisely what had to be denied and covered up by the conventional world. (Ibid., p. 366)

> Her past would not leave her even for the private affirmation of her value, and that past was murderous. Something like guilt seemed to suppress her voice. (Ibid., p. 371)

> Experience came toward her in either of two guises, one innocent and the other sinister . . . .But the rest of humankind [other than children and the very old] was fundamentally dangerous and had to be disarmed by a giving sexuality that was transfigured into a state beyond even feeling itself, a purely donative femininity. But that too could not sustain forever, for she meant to live at the peak always; only in the permanent rush of a crescendo was there safety, or at least forgetfulness, and when the wave dispersed she would turn cruelly against herself, so worthless, the scum of the earth, and her vileness would not let her sleep, and then the pills began and the little suicides each night. (Ibid., p. 436)

> She seemed able to see only that she had been victimized and betrayed by others, as though she were a mere passenger in her life . . . . All that was left was for her to go on defending her innocence, in which, at the bottom of her heart, she did not believe. Innocence kills. (Ibid., p. 484–485)

The reality of Marilyn Monroe's experience sears the reader. Her descent toward the Black Magician seems inexorable. She gave her love finally to no one but the druid named Dark who pulled her to her death. Monroe's childhood and teenage experience was doubly lethal because she was abused, molested, and raped and had no mother or adult she could tell or who cared about her. She had no one who could have, perhaps, mediated the trauma, comforted her, and brought the pattern to a halt. Monroe was alone. The immediacy of her experience, like the histories of my patients who were equally brutalized as children, is difficult to deal with. Perhaps this is why a fairy tale with its distancing, its "once long ago," makes a safer vehicle. Like a dream or series of dreams, the fairy tale can image reality in more digestible ways and both point to and be an indicator of healing.

Saeve, the maiden, and the chthonic feminine, Fionn and the Dark Druid can all be integrated in analysis. The healing takes place very slowly. The stages that I recognize, although not always in this order, are: the slow return of split-off memories and consciousness that the abuse happened (Saeve and the deer both get to know of each other's experiences); depression (the seven-year wandering in the deep woods); excoriating self-blame; full acknowledgment that she, as Saeve, was a victim and was not to blame, that even if she had had sexual feelings or was a sexy little girl or was told she was seductive, *she was not to blame* for what the druid did to her. Then comes understanding of the value of the sexual aspect of her femininity, that she deserved appreciation and encouragement of it, not its being seized from her and exploited for her powerful relative's use (Hillman (1987) examines this sensitively from a masculine viewpoint). With this realization, there comes embodiment, plus anger, rage, and blaming (the start of integration of valuable aspects of the dogs). There is a strong sense of outrage, with the projection of all the negative out onto others. Then, the slow integration of all the split-off parts, sometimes even of separate personalities, commences. Eventually there comes acknowledgment that one of these parts of her, alas, is the sadistic Dark Druid abuser and rapist whom she has internalized. Her greatest persecutor lives inside of her. The miracle is this inner figure's slow metamorphosis from the demonic bull masculine of the Dark Druid to its ecstatic form in the bull-god, Dionysus. Accompanying this process, both in dreams and in outer life, the woman starts asserting who she is and what she wants and needs and what she doesn't (as the dreamer in the Iphigeneia dream did in saying "No! No way!"). She no longer needs to hide or flee in panic as she had to as a child, like Saeve. Instead, she is entitled to both her waves of affect and their control. She is entitled to defend herself openly. Some of this, especially acknowledgment of the internal abuser, may not be possible. I have learned to be patient. Maybe the thing an abused woman needs most is for her therapist to wait and hold still. Pushing and probing, even penetrating interpretations, are experienced as further violations that need to be fled from. Each stage takes time and the full experience of each stage needs to be inhabited.

In my experience, grief comes with every stage and with every recovery of every fragmented piece. Maybe most of the work is grief work. Maybe most of any analysis is. I haven't said anything about the lacunae in memory. Did the experience happen as Saeve or the patient remembered it? Does she have the facts straight? Was it really a deer she turned into? Did she make it up, exaggerate? Was it one dog or two? Who is right: early or later Freud? I haven't said anything about this because, even though it matters intensely to my patient, at least while the animi villain and hero are persecuting her, truth to me is more in the psyche than in lawyers' proofs. And truth is in her story and in her symptoms and in her dreams whatever the specific particularities of the facts. Maybe as the dreams change and the fairy story develops, the future can change and shift what happened in the past. Then there's also psychological abuse and rape. There's what our culture shows its girl children and tells them about the feminine, how it says a maiden should behave. There's also the way our culture itself abuses and exploits the child/maiden, its Saeves and Marilyn Monroes. But I've gone on too long; I need to conclude my fairy tale.

A fter Saeve's son Oisin grew up, he was hunting one day with Bran and Sceolan when he came across the strangest sight: it was a woman with the head of a pig! It had happened that a king named Dubh (black) wanted no man to touch his daughter nor marry her so he, himself, touched her with a druid's rod and got a pig's head upon her in place of her own. This pig-headed woman hunted alongside Oisin and helped carry his game and hers and ran and worked beside him. They grew very hot and she opened her robe to cool herself. When Oisin saw her body's beauty he commiserated with her. She said if he'd marry her, the spell would be broken. He did and she regained her head and all her beauty (Curtin 1890).

Much later, though, Osian followed in his mother's footsteps. He wandered into fairyland with another fairy maid and got lost for centuries, but that is another story.

A distant relative, because all druids are related, was Lady Ragnell whose half-brother was Lord Gromer, the son of the female druid, Morgan le Fay. (I have primarily used versions of the grail legend told by Loomis (1956), Phelps (1981), and Whitmont (1982).) The villainous Gromer changed his sister, Ragnell, into a loathsome old crone because she wouldn't give her love to him. Sir Gawain broke the spell. He not only married her, but accepted her as she was, even bedding the hag. This broke half the spell and she turned back into a maiden. The rest of the spell lifted when he gave her back her sovereignty: her own power over herself. He left it to her to decide if and when she'd be beautiful or ugly, maiden or crone. Now, if you read these texts carefully, nothing is there to imply she *has* to turn beautiful and stay that way as a Kore, repressing the Crone. That's only a cultural misreading that's been around for a few hundred years or so. These three fairy tales point the way toward the reuniting of opposites and toward the feminine in all of us gaining access to all parts of herself — maiden, mother, crone. She would not give her love to the druid named Dark because she's trying to keep it for all parts of her many-sided Self. Then, from that center, she can be capable of a true relationship with an accurately seen, complicated, other human being. But that, my dears, is a never ending story that, with any luck, takes a lifetime.

REFERENCES

Bettelheim, B. 1977. *The Uses of Enchantment: The Meaning and Importance of Fairy Tales.* New York: Random House.

Bly, R. 1986. *Fairy Tales for Men and Women.* Recording. St. Paul, Minn.: Ally Press Center.

Butler, S. 1978. *Conspiracy of Silence: The Trauma of Incest.* San Francisco: Volcano Press.

Cavendish, R., ed. 1970. Druids. In *Man, Myth and Magic: Illustrated Encyclopedia of the Supernatural*, vol. 6. New York: Marshall Cavendish Co., pp. 718–723.

Cirlot, J. E. 1982. *A Dictionary of Symbols.* New York: Philosophical Library.

Cooper, J. 1978. *An Illustrated Encyclopedia of Traditional Symbols.* London: Thames and Hudson Ltd.

Curtin, J. 1890. *Myths and Folk Tales of Ireland.* New York: Dover, 1975.

Evans-Wentz, W. Y. 1966. *The Fairy Faith in Celtic Countries.* Oxford: University Books Inc.

Forward, S., and Buck, C. 1984. *Betrayal of Innocence: Incest and Devastation.* New York: Penguin Books.

Frankfort, H. 1978. *Kingship and the Gods.* Chicago: University of Chicago Press.

Gilbert, S., and Gubar, S. 1980. *The Madwoman in the Attic: The Woman Writer and the Nineteenth-Century Imagination.* New Haven, Conn.: Yale University Press.

Graves, R. 1951. *The White Goddess*. New York: Farrar, Straus and Giroux.

_____. 1960. *The Greek Myths*, vol. 2. New York: Viking Penguin Inc.

Haddon, C. P. 1987. Delivering yang-femininity. In *Spring* (1987): 133–143.

Hannah, B. 1954. *Cat, Dog and Horse Seminar*. Lectures given at the C. G. Jung Institute, Zurich.

Herman, J., and Hirschman, L. 1977. Father–daughter incest. In *Signs* 2, 4: 735–756.

Hillman, J. 1987. A psychology of transgression drawn from an incest dream. *Spring* (1987): 66–76.

Jobes, G. 1962. *Dictionary of Mythology, Folklore and Symbols*. New York: Scarecrow Press.

Jung, C. G. 1951. The psychological aspects of the Kore. In *Collected Works* 9i:182–206. Princeton, N.J.: Princeton University Press, 1959.

_____. 1948. The phenomenology of the spirit in fairy tales. In *Collected Works* 9i:207–254. Princeton, N.J.: Princeton University Press, 1959.

_____. 1955–1956. *Mysterium Coniunctionis. Collected Works*, vol. 14. Princeton N.J.: Princeton University Press, 1963.

Kennedy, P. 1866. *Legendary Fictions of the Celts*. London: Macmillan and Co.

Kerenyi, C. 1978. *The Gods of the Greeks*. London: Thames and Hudson.

Koltuv, B. B. 1986. *The Book of Lilith*. York Beach, Maine: Nicolas Hays.

Loomis, R. S. 1956. *Wales and the Arthurian Legend*. Cardiff: University of Wales Press.

Miller, A. 1987. *Timebends*. New York: Grove Press.

Neumann, E. 1970. *The Origins and History of Consciousness*. Princeton, N.J.: Princeton University Press.

Norton-Taylor, D. 1974. *The Celts* New York: Time Inc.

Phelps, E. L. 1981. *The Maid of the North*. New York: Holt, Rinehart and Winston.

Perera, S. 1986. *Challenges of the Celtic Goddesses*. Lecture at the C. G. Jung Institute of New York.

Piggott, S. 1987. *The Druids*. New York: Thames and Hudson.

Renvoize, J. 1982. *Incest: A Family Pattern*. London: Routledge and Kegan Paul Ltd.

Russell, D. 1986. *The Secret Trauma: Incest in the Lives of Girls and Women*. New York: Basic Books Inc.

Rolleston, T. W. 1911. *Myths and Legends of the Irish Race*. London: George Harrap and Co. Ltd.

Stephens, J. 1920. *Irish Fairy Tales*. London: Macmillan and Co. Ltd.

Tatar, M. 1987. *The Hard Facts of the Grimms' Fairy Tales*. Princeton, N.J.: Princeton University Press.

von Franz, M.-L. 1976. *The Feminine in Fairy Tales*. Zurich: Spring Publications.

———. 1980. *Shadow and Evil in Fairy Tales*. Dallas: Spring Publications.

Whitmont, E. C. 1982. *Return of the Goddess*. New York: Crossroad.

Wilde, L. 1899. *Ancient Legends Mystic Charms and Superstitions of Ireland*. London: Chatto and Windus.

"Rapunzel"
Barrenness and Bounty,
Differentiation and Reconciliation

T. J. Kapacinskas and Judith A. Robert

This is a reflection, a reverie, upon the story of "Rapunzel" (Manheim 1977, pp. 46–49). Our imagining into the story is an invitation to the reader to "hold" the images or to allow oneself to be "held" by them, allowing the flow of associated material to unfold. This is a way of making the story more "ample." Thus, one may follow Jung who says that "the nature of the psyche. . .consists of reflected images" and thereby seek to discern how it is that psyche shows itself in these story images (Jung 1926, par. 610). This reflection utilizes a way in, like the little windows in the story, and breaks off arbitrarily.

Rapunzel

Once upon a time there was a husband and wife who had long wished for a child and who finally believed their wish might be granted. One day as the wife looked out of her little window she spied some rapunzel, a kind of lettuce, in a garden behind the house. She craved the rapunzel but there was a high wall around the garden which no one dared enter as it belonged to a witch whose power everyone feared. The wife longed for the rapunzel and her craving grew each day. She began to waste away as she knew she would never get any. Finally, her husband, worried that his wife might die, stole into the garden at night to get her a handful of the lettuce. But her craving increased threefold the next day and her husband again returned to the garden at night. But this time he was caught by the witch! He pleaded for his life, saying that he only did it for his wife who would die without some rapunzel. Hearing this, the witch agreed to let him have all the rapunzel he wished on condition that he give her the child when it was born. The frightened husband agreed and when the baby was born the witch named her Rapunzel and took her away.

Rapunzel grew to be "the loveliest child under the sun." When she was twelve the witch locked her in a tower with no doors and only a little window at the top deep within the forest. At evening the witch would come to visit, calling out: "Rapunzel, Rapunzel, let down your hair for me." Rapunzel would let down her golden hair and the witch would climb up.

One day a prince was riding through the forest and heard Rapunzel singing in her loneliness. Enchanted, he looked for a door into the tower but could find none and rode away. Yet his heart had been touched and he returned every day to listen. Once, as he stood behind a tree, he saw the witch come to the tower and call out, and he thereby learned the secret. The next day he went to the tower and called, "Rapunzel, Rapunzel, let down your hair for me." The prince climbed up and when she first saw him, Rapunzel was frightened for she had never seen a man. But he calmed her saying he had been touched by her singing. He then asked her if she would marry him and she agreed, thinking that the prince would love her more than her godmother, the witch. Rapunzel then made a plan whereby the prince would bring skeins of silk everyday when he came to visit and she would weave a ladder to escape.

But one day Rapunzel said to the witch, "Tell me, Godmother, how is it that you're so much harder to pull up than the young prince?" The witch was furious at the betrayal, and she angrily cut off Rapunzel's hair and sent her to a desert to live in misery. When the prince returned and called out to Rapunzel, the witch let down the hair and he climbed up. The angry witch threatened to scratch out his eyes as she told him that Rapunzel was gone. In despair, the prince leapt from the tower and the brambles scratched his eyes and blinded him.

The prince wandered through the forest for several years weeping over the loss of his wife. One day he came to the desert place where Rapunzel was living with the twins she had borne him, a boy and a girl. She took him in her arms, whereupon her tears fell into his eyes and he could see again. The prince then took his family to his kingdom where they lived happily for years to come.

INTRODUCTION

In the initial image of "Rapunzel," two feminine figures, "wife" and "witch" have been walled-off from each other. This separation has permitted differentiation of each. On one side there is a wife with a devoted husband and, on the other side of the wall, a witch with a marvelous garden. But the "walling-off" has thrown a long shadow—the wife is barren and cannot flower forth, and the witch is isolated with her abundant resources. Thus, this differentiation also brings suffering. We can imagine that the wife would like to be fruitful like the witch's plants seen through her little window and that the witch would like to hand on to the next generation her skills and knowledge, but she is without relationship and faces death without issue.

The husband tries to bring about a connection between his wife's craving and the witch's abundance. But his invasive attempt to pilfer the witch's rapunzel constellates rapaciousness in the witch, who snatches the couple's child.

Rapunzel, who serves an apprenticeship to the witch, and who later becomes a wife and mother, effects a reconciliation of wife and witch within herself.

These "feminine" energies belong to the common pool of human experience, not just to women. Energy that "wifes" might exist in a man. Certainly women "husband" through some "masculinity" of their own. Denotations of masculinity and femininity are not hard-and-fast categories proper to only one sex. Therefore, our invitation is to polymorphousness in reflective style, to see how these images belong to all of us. To amplify them we have drawn upon the imaginings of our cultural heritage in ancient Greek myth. But it is useful to remember that mythic personifications from any tradition might do as well.

THE COUPLE'S BARRENNESS

Our fairy tale begins after a man and woman have long wished for a child and now believe their wish will come true. This pair has been barren—without fruit—and although this is about to change, a reflection on this condition of barrenness provides a contrast with that of the witch. Our couple has not been able to give form and substance to their aspiration for life. We are reminded of the mythic image of barrenness in the Homeric hymn to Demeter (Boer 1979, pp. 90–135). For our Greek ancestors, Demeter, the goddess of agricultural vegetation, imaged the cultivated fecundity of the earth. Alienation from "she who feeds many" would result not only in the loss of the earth's fertility but also death without issue, the fate our couple long endured (Lincoln 1981, p. 76). As the hymn puts it:

> And she made this the most terrible year on this earth that feeds so many, and the most cruel. The earth did not take seed that year, for Demeter in her beautiful crown concealed it. And the cattle many times pulled their bent ploughs in vain over the land, and many times the white barley fell uselessly upon the earth. And in fact she would have wiped out the whole race of talking men with a painful famine. (Boer 1979, p. 118)

Modern consciousness may find it difficult to grasp the symbolism of the couple's desire for a child. In the media there are juxtapositions of opposing images. Images of "in vitro" fertilization are followed by images of starving children in famine-stricken countries. Images of organ transplants prolonging life are followed by statistics portending an overpopulated earth. Although we are awash with oppositions, we are captured by the plight of a child trapped in a well, surviving an air crash, abandoned, or abused. The "child" strikes a deep chord within each of us. As Jung says:

> The "child" is born out of the womb of the unconscious, begotten out of the depths of human nature, or rather out of living Nature herself. It is a personification of vital forces quite outside the limited range of our conscious mind; of ways and possibilities of which our one-sided conscious mind knows nothing; a wholeness which embraces the very depths of Nature. It represents the strongest, the most ineluctable urge in every being, namely the urge to realize itself. It is, as it were, and incarnation of *the inability to do otherwise*, equipped with all the power of nature and instinct, whereas the conscious mind is always getting caught up in its supposed ability to do otherwise. (1951, par. 289)

Since the child is the "personification of vital forces," the urge to self-realization, no child would mean no ability to incarnate new possibilities for the renewal of life.

So it is poignant when the mother in our story conceives but begins to "waste away" saying: "I shall die unless I get some rapunzel to eat from the garden behind our house." Her death also means the death of the child. The mother experiences an inner lack, a hunger within, which must be filled if she and the child are to survive. This is a longing for the spirit of Demeter, "she who feeds many," in the form of the rapunzel the mother craves. Let us turn now to its symbolism.

The root "rap" found in the word *rapunzel* functions with many imagistic resonances. "Rap" imitates the penetrating (as in rapier) sound of striking which has to do not only with knocks at a door but blows struck while seizing and snatching (*rapax*, rape). An example is the rapacious penetration of the witch's garden and theft of her plants; or, the witch's snatching of the child, Rapunzel, from her parents. "Rap" also refers to a one-hundred-twenty-yard skein such as the silk with which Rapunzel and the prince hope to escape the tower. "Rap" is phonetically clustered with "rab" of kohl rabi, and the plants of the cabbage, turnip, and radish families. The cabbage, with its graceful curling leaves, is reminiscent of the vulva's labia and old wives' tales that babies come from heads of cabbage. Since the rab or rap of Rapunzel is also a radish, varying as radishes do from being long and white or purple, to red and plump, the implicit nuances suggest both phallic, earth-penetrating rhizomes and succulent, protruding breasts. The clusters of meaning around "rapunzel" are rich in the imagery of rapaciousness, sexuality, and nurturance (Klein 1971, pp. 616–617).

Rapunzel, or rampion, a variety of lettuce, is ruled astrologically by the moon, an ancient symbol of the mother and maternal nurturance. The word *lettuce* is derived from words which mean milk, alluding to the milky juice of the lettuce plant (ibid., p. 418). Rose suggests that "eaten often it will increase the flow of milk in a nursing mother" (1972, p. 76). Thus the mother-to-be craves the milky nurturance of lettuce, mother's milk, that she might nurture. But this desired nurturance is to be found in the witch's garden.

Mythically, we see that the sustaining spirit of Demeter and of Hecate, goddess of nursing, have been absent. How can she, who has not been nurtured, nurture? Such a dilemma might be experienced in relationship, community, or creative work when a man or woman has not been nurtured and therefore does not know how to give nurturance or sustain it. On a larger scale, the image of nurturance within our culture appears wounded. Many children are exploited and abused. Much art, architecture, and city planning does not sustain but surrounds with dehumanized ugliness.

THE WITCH AND HER BOUNTIFUL GARDEN

The fecund world of feminine nurturance is controlled by the witch who possesses a "wonderful garden, full of beautiful flowers and vegetables." There is a tradition that witches are descendants of priestesses of the Great Goddess, retaining many powers delegated by her, including knowledge of vegetation and use of herbs of all kinds (DeVries 1974, p. 504). From ancient times, witches were recognized as healers and poisoners since the same herbs that cure can be poisonous in larger amounts. *Venefica*, or female poisoner in Latin, came to be the word for witch in most romance languages. Yet for much of history, witches were the only physicians available to the poor. Witches discovered herbal treatments such as digitalis for heart disease, ephedrine for hay fever and asthma, ergonovine and atropine used in childbirthing (Jong 1981, p. 141).

Thus, the witch is revered for healing knowledge and feared for destructive power. Like Demeter she can produce bounty or barrenness; like Hecate she commands "knowledge of enchanting herbs" and "how to prepare poisons and antidotes" (Kerenyi 1979, p. 33). While the wife longs for the nurturance the witch possesses, she and her husband fear the witch. Symmetrically, the witch fears worldly intrusion on her garden but cannot produce a child by herself.

Both parties view each other suspiciously, refuse relationship, and do not attempt to understand each other. Each incarnates a specific "energy" in isolation. This lack of relationship images in the high wall. Such a walling-off denies or hides from consciousness a wounded place, a lack of development, or sensitivity of which one is protective. One may fear shame, judgment, or being labeled as evil. Nonetheless, Jung argued, the neglected side of life, or "shadow," makes itself felt. Thus, the wife must eventually reckon with the witch and she with the wife.

> Unfortunately there can be no doubt that man is, on the whole, less good than he imagines himself or wants to be. Everyone carries a shadow, and the less it is embodied in the individual's conscious life, the blacker and denser it is. If an inferiority is con-

scious, one always has a chance to correct it. Furthermore, it is constantly in contact with other interests, so that it is continually subjected to modifications. But if it is repressed and isolated from consciousness, it never gets corrected, and is liable to burst forth suddenly in a moment of unawareness. (Jung 1937, par. 131)

In isolation from the witch, the wife has pursued relationship to a male thereby devoting herself to Hera, guardian of marriage. "The cult of Hera. . .was tied. . .to the time of wedding, [and] to the times in the feminine life cycle. . .which made possible or impossible the encounter between wife and husband" (Kerenyi 1978, p. 6). In contrast, the witch has eschewed mating and her reproductive energy has flowed to plants and herbs, a bondedness to Demeter and Hecate. Our story opens where these bifurcated paths now intersect and unless they cross-fertilize, both will die without issue.

THE CRAVING FOR RAPUNZEL

The wife's craving sets our story in motion. To "crave" means "to ask," or demand what is desired (Klein 1971, pp. 174, 200). "Desire" is composed of "de" meaning *from*, and "sideris" meaning *star*. Desire, then, is "from the stars" or to "expect from the stars" (ibid., p. 205). To understand what is timely in the desires of mankind, astrology is mindful of the movement of the heavens. So the wife's desire for the witch's rapunzel suggests that it is time (from the stars) for the wife to contact the witch.

The wife's desire for the rapunzel increases when she tastes it, it does not diminish. That the craving intensifies upon consumption indicates that is it not merely a physical hunger. The craving is symbolic of an inner lack, the missing Demeter/Hecate spirit, which desire seeks to remedy by breaching the wall and bridging the separation between wife and witch. This compulsion is "the inability to do otherwise" of which Jung spoke in discussing the child archetype. Indeed it is the hungry child within the mother that cannot let the wife do other than contact the witch.

This image of insatiable, greedy, or compulsive hunger appears in the mythology of the goddess Demeter. She has the power to curse one with hunger as well as satisfy. In one tale, she curses Eryischthon to suffer perpetual hunger. He invades one of her sacred groves, felling trees for his banqueting halls. Demeter appears as priestess of the grove and orders him to desist. He threatens her with his axe and she curses him to suffer perpetual hunger, no matter how much he eats. In the Homeric hymn in her honor, the inconsolable Demeter refuses to take sustenance for nine days and nights. When she is offered barley water, Abas cries, "Oh, how greedily you drink!" and is turned into a lizard by her harsh glance (Graves 1960, sec. 24). Thus, this goddess brings experiences of insatiable or greedy hunger, such as the wife suffers, when her gifts are refused or her domain dishonored.

Today we might speak of the wife's compulsive desire as a form of addiction. In an addiction, the body craves a food, substance, or activity (perhaps sex or gambling), and the acting out of the desire intensifies the craving. Addict and addiction come from the Latin roots "ad," meaning *to* or *from*, coupled with "dicere," meaning *to say* (Klein 1971, p. 11). Hence the "addict" is one who acts from what is "said" and thus, what is "heard" as command. To understand addiction, we must listen to the commands that we "hear" metaphorically. What is the symbolic nature of the desire craving expression? What inner "child" seeks realization? Symbolic understanding of the desire and the attempt to come to terms with it on a different level can help curb the embodied craving.

Jung emphasized this idea in his letter to William G. Wilson, the founder of Alcoholics Anonymous, when he wrote:

> craving for alcohol. . .[is] the equivalent on a low level of the spiritual thirst of our being for wholeness, expressed in medieval language: the union with God. . . .[A]lcohol in Latin is *spiritus* and you use the same word for the highest religious experience as well as for the most depraving poison. The helpful formula therefore is: *spiritus contra spiritum.* (Jung 1973, pp. 624–625)

The wife enacts her desire through the eating of the rapunzel. The "spirit" of this act intoxicates her and she is unable to resist gratifying her desire on the literal level. There is no *spiritus contra spiritum* – nothing to go against the raw physical craving. She seeks the special consciousness of Demetrian spirit through the witch's rapunzel. But how else might the wife and husband honor the Goddess whose imperative she hears?

Here we must remember that Demeter's gifts to mankind are twofold: the crops, which nourish the body, *and* the feminine mysteries of initiation, which sustain the soul (Kerenyi 1977, pp. 15, 121). Since, in our story, the wife and husband do not have their own garden, the wife might enact her longing in Demetrian rituals expressing a connection with the rhythms of nature and the cultivation of mother–daughter relationships (Jung 1951, par. 316–317). She may also benefit from rituals involving Hecate's knowledge of herbs and nursing. Examples of such rituals include those of Demeter at Eleusis, Ariadne at the Villa of Mysteries, May Day festivals, and initiation ceremonies. The meaning of such rituals is described in the words of a contemporary Mescalaro Apache who says of their puberty ceremony that it brings about "a reunion with the primary life force" so that "our women folk will continue to bring forth strong and healthy children and. . .we will continue to live as a people" (Farrer 1987, p. 241). These rituals provide a liturgical, symbolic embodiment in song and movement that may satisfy the need to connect with spirit while minimizing the destructiveness in more literal forms of gratification. However, in many cultures such rituals no longer exist or fail those who once believed. But understanding their purpose may assist in constructing new rituals to ease spiritual hunger.

James Hillman discusses the way in which a compulsion might be transformed in his essay on Pan. Mythically, Pan rules sexual compulsions such as rape and masturbation which can have a panicky quality. In one story, Pan desires Syrinx, a nymph, who, in order to escape him, changes herself into a reed in the river. Pan then transforms the reed she has become into the syrinx – Pan's pipes, i.e., shepherd's pipes – which he then plays. Says Hillman:

> In the Syrinx tale Pan pursues the possibility of reflection, which by ever-receding, transforms into its instrument. The music of the Syrinx is the self-consciousness that inhibits and transforms the compulsion. Instead of rape on the river-bank, there is plaintive piping, song and dance. The compulsion is not sublimated, however, but expressed in and through another image, for song and dance are also instinctual. Through the syrinx the noise which Pan is fond of becomes music, the tumult, a measured step; patterns elaborate; there is space, distance and air, like the soughing of the wind in the pine. . . .
>
> These tales tell us that instinctual nature itself desires that which would make it aware of itself. No new principle is introduced, no corrective of compulsion from above or outside the configuration of Pan himself. He seeks an intangible light, the muse's nurse – a helpful awareness through the dark of concretistic sexuality and panic. Pan tells us that the strongest longing of nature

"in here" (and maybe 'out there' as well) is towards union with itself in awareness. . . .The other whom Pan chases so compulsively is none other than himself reflected, transposed to another key. (Hillman 1972, p. xlix)

Pan's way of wrestling with compulsion is to pursue the reflection of it in music and dance: to stay with the compulsion in an embodied way and take it to a different level. This accomplishes the same kind of spiritual containment that play, games, and liturgical rituals seek to approximate in their activities and festivals of song and dance, poetry and drama.

The wife and husband hear the "rap at the door" of Demeter and Hecate but resist deepening into the desire either because of laziness (no garden of their own), personal ignorance (lack of knowledge of rituals), or cultural prejudice (contempt for the witch). They are caught in the "supposed ability to do otherwise," of which Jung spoke, pursuing the satisfaction of the physical craving by stealing the rapunzel.

CONFRONTING THE WITCH

Crossing the wall at night and stealing the rapunzel leads to a confrontation with the witch, a theophany of the Goddess Hecate, whose domain is the nocturnal "crossroads." She is the darker, frightening aspect of the lunar goddess triad: the waxing, waning, and dark moons, associated with Demeter, Persephone, and Hecate; mother, maiden, and crone. Hecate commands "the most secret knowledge of exits and entries, of life's origin and its termination (Kerenyi 1979, p. 33). She was honored by the priestess Medea, who was known as a "child-concealer. . . .Her's is the place of dismemberment, of cutting up and dispersing the living, of murder" (ibid., pp. 32–33).

It is this side of Hecate that the husband encounters in the witch. "She is either exceedingly beautiful or horribly ugly; bewitching in her physical graces or terrifyingly hideous" (Jong 1981, p. 66). Her seductiveness may arouse erections and wet dreams and her power the dread of impotence (ibid., p. 108). At once she embodies the beauty and hideousness of nature.

Although the husband is overcome by the witch, the tale of Perseus slaying Medusa gives an example of how to approach such power. Liz Greene suggests that Medusa embodies the anger and hatred of violated femininity which — if looked at directly — petrifies and renders one impotent. The gods give Perseus the "capacity for reflection, for symbolic thinking," which enables him to succeed (Greene 1984, p. 230). From Hades – via the Stygian Nymphs – comes the invisibility that permits him to get close, more deeply "into" Medusa's rage. Athene's shield provides the reflection that enables Perseus to approach indirectly and utilize Hermes' differentiating sickle to behead Medusa. The power of rage is transformed as Medusa's head is separated from her body and Pegasus springs forth – instinct takes wing! But the husband in our story is not Perseus, he does not reflect, and upon encountering the witch, he promises her the child.

This rapacious attempt to steal the rapunzel also takes us into the realm of Hermes, messenger of the gods, who, like Hecate, patronizes crossings. Hermes is called "the Thief," commemorating his notorious theft of Apollo's cattle. When he is apprehended (his message grasped), Hermes makes connections. Unwittingly, the panicky husband brings about a hermetic connection between couple and witch when he is caught.

The husband's foray into the witch's garden is countered by the witch's theft of the child. How are we to understand such rapaciousness? The witch is contained within her flourishing garden, resisting intrusion by others and the rituals of mating, thereby foregoing generation of a child. He who can father can only enter her "garden" as a thief. What the witch has cultivated, all the nurturant capacities and power, cannot of itself result in the birth of a child. Yet she, too, is governed by the deepest of natural laws, the "strongest. . .most ineluctable urge. . .the urge to realize. . .[her]self" (Jung 1951, par. 289), but she will have no successor if the situation does not change. Witches were adherents of ancient, nonproselytizing fertility cults; yet without disciples knowledge could not be passed on and the witch's "kingdom" renewed (Jong 1981, pp. 62–63). Thus, we can imagine the witch's delight when she hears that the wife craves rapunzel. This desire communicates to the vegetation-wise witch that the wife is pregnant and she can bargain for the renewal that is at hand.

The witch's unlived desire to have a child, pupil, and successor is repressed and "shadowy"; it comes out in her rapacious "snatching" of the couple's child. This Hecatean tendency to snatch and conceal a child is not, as Jung put it, "constantly in contact with other interests. . .continually subjected to modifications" so it "burst[s] forth suddenly" (Jung 1937, par. 131). The witch, like the couple, literalizes her desire – no social ritualization of her need, no patient gathering of pupils. She must have the flesh-and-blood baby now!

The couple and the witch partake of the "resistant world of matter," each resisting the divine power mediated through the other. The witch needs regeneration on the human level just as the couple needs fertility on the vegetative level. Each requires and constellates the other.

> Rape [or rapaciousness] shows the compulsive necessity within and behind all generation. The closer one is to the world of material nature, the more sexual and compulsive will the divine power show itself. Rape is the paradigm for the divine penetration and fecundation of the resistant world of matter. (Hillman 1972, pp. xxxvi–xxxvii)

Our mature pregnant woman may fear old age and death even as she covets the fruits of an old wise woman. Conversely, the death-conscious crone is secretive and avaricious with her knowledge even as she envies the mature woman's capacity to mate and give birth.

The separating wall is a "party wall" erected by both sides out of fear. The shunned witch fears persecution as well as suppression of her knowledge by the collective community, while the couple exhibits the Judeo-Christian fear of the power of nature whose representative is the witch. As an inner dilemma, such a situation might be felt as a fear of reconciling family or community demands with inner experience which nourishes.

For these resistant figures to be open to each other would mean a relationship with the shadow as carried by the other: a process of overcoming fear while acknowledging the value in what is called "evil." Holding the tension of opposites of these twin energies in her soul is what the child Rapunzel's destiny comes to be.

RAPUNZEL'S APPRENTICESHIP TO THE WITCH

When the witch claims the baby and names her Rapunzel another Hecatean crossroads is reached. Like Demeter, with whom she was "closely associated in ritual," Hecate was a goddess of fertility but was also noted for "Zeus [having] made her nurse of the young" (Tripp 1970, p. 261). We can imagine the witch nursing and caring for baby Rapunzel with the assiduousness of Hecate who helped the grieving Demeter search out her lost Kore.

Psychologically it may be that when the birth crossroads is reached, a different energy takes over in a woman – the Hecatean archetype. This energy is devoted to nursing the child, the healing knowledge of herbs, and the awareness of "poisons and antidotes" (Kerenyi 1979, p. 33). With such Demetrian/Hecatean bonding, a daughter may become her mother's pupil with whom she is loathe to part.

This fear of parting may underlie the witch's concealing of Rapunzel in the tower which echos the practice of concealing children in Hera's temple during her annual celebrations in Corinth. Children were kept for a year in Hera's temple, as though in exile or dead, to confer immortality, imitating the disappearing children of Medea, Hecate's priestess (ibid., pp. 30–40). Thus parting of mother and child at death would be only temporary. The relationship between Hera, guardian of marriage, and Hecate, patroness of "life's origin and. . .termination," emphasizes the connection between marriage, childbirth, and death. It may help us to understand why we encounter these separate but *sub rosa* connected figures – wife–mother, witch–nurse, and child.

Rapunzel is locked in the tower at the age of twelve, the puberty transition from childhood to adolescence. At this time the sexuality of the child blossoms in physical changes and increasing attraction to the opposite sex, as an identity separate from parental figures emerges. The witch, who cannot stop this process, hopes to control it and keep Rapunzel unconscious of it by hiding her in the tower deep within the forest. This repeats an underlying theme: the tendency to split off or wall off. A contemporary version may be forbidding daughters to date until a certain age or sending them to a girls' boarding school, the "ivory tower" of higher learning, where education seeks to channel and civilize instinct.

The witch gained access to the tower by calling out: "Rapunzel, Rapunzel, let down your hair for me." Rapunzel would unbind her braided hair and fasten it to the window latch for leverage, enabling the witch to climb up.

Here the story reprises an important motif: the little window without which nothing happens. Rapunzel's mother had only a little window to gaze into the witch's garden. Rapunzel has only a little window through which she achieves intercourse with the world utilizing her hair and song. "[T]he Roman *porta fenestrella* [was] a special opening through which Fortune passed, and the word window (fenestra) 'was used symbolically in the sense of "opening," "opportunity" ' " (Hillman 1979, p. 152; see also Onians 1953, p. 348). The "window of opportunity" enables both mother and daughter to move beyond their confining walls.

Rapunzel's beautiful long hair signifies the emergence of her sexual fecundity and creative power under the tutelage of the witch: overflowing, like the witch's abundant garden. Its braiding signifies the channeling of her potency. "Tantric sages declared that the binding or unbinding of women's hair activated cosmic forces of creation and destruction," controlled by goddesses such as Isis, Cybele, and Kali (Walker 1983, p. 368). Since "[f]or the sun gods, hair represented both 'rays' and virility," Rapunzel's golden hair suggests strength, both in the weight-bearing capacity of her hair and in the power to endure which she evinces (ibid., p. 370).

Rapunzel reconciles the experience of the witch *and* the mother kept split by the prior generation. Like the witch for whom she lets down her hair, the virginal Rapunzel belongs partly to Demeter and Hecate, and, untouched by masculinity, she honors these goddesses with her creativity.

The witch is like Demeter, who would keep Kore forever at her side. In the *Hymn to Demeter* the conspiracy of Zeus, Hades, and Gaia is necessary to enable Kore to escape her overly nurturant mother. "Hades rape of the innocent soul is a central necessity for psychic change" (Hillman 1975, p. 208). Rapunzel, too, must be "taken" if she is to experience that in her soul which is different from the witch.

The tower symbolizes both the witch's fear of losing Rapunzel and that which brings about the loss. The witch locks Rapunzel in the tower to shut her "away from the world." Ironically, this phallic tower calls attention to Rapunzel and her one-sided development. In her isolation and loneliness Rapunzel develops a beautiful, enchanting voice which gives expression to her longing. From the high tower her song floats melancholy and melodious through the forest like an advertisement for all to hear. She projects her soul into the world with her voice and captivates the prince.

Rapunzel "tempts" and enchants the prince with her song just as Kore draws forth Hades from the underworld when she reaches for the bloom of the Narcissus. Both suggest that narcissistic fascination, autoerotic desire, evokes the "other" who brings about change. Narcissistic enchantment prepares one to fall in love. Through desire part of one's self "falls" for the other and it is as if one is carried away as Kore by Hades, or Rapunzel by the prince. First we imagine, then see ourselves in others, projecting the soul outward, and then, through the process of reflection, we reclaim ourselves.

The prince's heart is so touched by the singing that he returns every day until he learns the witch's secret means of entry. At nightfall he repeats the witch's formula and gains entrance to the tower, where he calms Rapunzel's fears and she consents to marry him. "[W]hat happens during the moment love is born: the woman cannot resist the voice calling forth her terrified soul; the man cannot resist the woman whose soul thus responds to his voice" (Kundera 1984, p. 160). As Rapunzel needs a different order if her life is to change, the prince needs a partner to realize himself, to be fruitful.

SECRET WORLDS END

Rapunzel keeps her relationship with the prince a secret from the witch. Whereas her parents denied a place for the witch in their lives, Rapunzel has an ongoing relationship with her. But marriage then falls into shadow for Rapunzel. She cannot relate openly to the husband-prince as the relationship is relegated to the night-world.

This problem is instructive as to how "shadow" falls. The witch, as the mother's shadow, may be that aspect of femininity that takes over at Rapunzel's birth and becomes her primary experience of "mothering." But because Rapunzel's mother denies her "witchiness," Rapunzel, too, would sense that this part of herself ought to be kept hidden, in shadow. Nevertheless, the Hecatean-witchy side of mother is actually in charge, pushing the Hera-relating mode into shadow for Rapunzel. Rapunzel is thus faced with a twin problem: how to acknowledge both the witch and wife dimensions of herself. With the onset of puberty she might feel even more "locked in" if she is unable to realize either her Demetrian/Hecatean or Hera dimensions in the world.

Rapunzel devises a plan of escape from the tower: a ladder made from skeins of silk which the prince is to bring on his daily visits. Schooled in the witch's arts, Rapunzel is confident that she can weave the "raps" of silk, the product of cultivated silk worms, into a ladder of escape. Like her parents, the new couple hopes to avoid confronting the witch, as the prince "takes" Rapunzel secretly against the witch's will. Escape down a ladder made from "raps" of silk may image both the "taking" and the hoped-for smooth transition.

Rapunzel and her prince create a private world in the tower each evening high up off the ground emphasizing its dreamlike quality. It is like the early relationship of Eros and Psyche. Psyche, confined to Eros's palace, is visited at night by Eros whom she never sees in daylight. This dreamy situation continues until another enters by accident. Seeking to glimpse him, Psyche spills hot oil from a lamp on the sleeping Eros, shocking him into awareness, and he flutters away. Intimacy is only reestablished with great suffering to both. Rapunzel's naive remark to the witch – "Tell me, Godmother, how is it that you're so much harder to pull up than the young prince? With him it hardly takes a minute" – ends her secret world with the prince. Betrayal of the witch ends the couple's innocence as they are thrust out of the garden.

The witch cannot initiate Rapunzel into the path of relationship and motherhood. Life with the witch gives Rapunzel a good registry of the heaviness (weight) of the witch's path in life. But the witch deprives Rapunzel of initiation into relationship and the burdens of being a wife and mother. So it is that the prince is "light" and easy to pull up. When thrust out by the witch, pregnant and alone, Rapunzel acquires initiation into the heaviness of the marital path (Kundera 1984, p. 160).

We are as chagrined by Rapunzel's remark as we are disappointed in Psyche for giving in to her envious sisters' demands that she "see" Eros. Yet both "mistakes" are necessary to reveal the cost of relatedness. As Jung says: "If you avoid error you do not live, and one often gets to truth through error" (Jung 1977, p. 98).

The witch is outraged when she learns that her secret world with Rapunzel has been violated. In high dudgeon, she presents the angry, vengeful side of Hecate, a wild dog at a crossroads, seizing Rapunzel's hair, snapping off the long braids in the jaws of her scissors, and thrusting her out into the world. Her "dismemberment" of the secret world of Rapunzel and the prince echos the abandoned Medea's "dispersing the living" in her role as Hecate's priestess. Cutting Rapunzel's hair initiates her into womanhood, symbolically "concealing" the child and bringing forth the woman. Hair-cutting and making an offering of it at puberty is a ritual practice based on the association of hair growth with the coming of sexual vigor and generative power

(Onians 1953, pp. 231–232). The witch's Hecatean/Demetrian knowledge of nature tells her that Rapunzel is pregnant, as she knew earlier that Rapunzel's mother had conceived. In this act of cutting the hair and casting her out, the witch symbolically enacts a rite of passage for the adolescent woman, Rapunzel. Today, women continue to observe this ritual, unknowingly, as they often change hairstyle after the birth of a child. Stern notes that mother–infant observation has shown "that during the first year after the infant's birth a large number of mothers go through a great number of drastic changes in hair style as they seek out their new identity" (1985, p. 186).

Similarly, the witch shocks the prince when she turns on him like Demeter turns on Abas when she has lost Kore, metamorphosing him into a lizard with an angry glance. The witch says to the prince, "The bird is gone from the nest, she won't be singing any more; the cat has taken her away and before she's done she'll scratch your eyes out too." Rather than waiting to see what might emerge from a woman become a force of nature, the prince leaps for his life. In leaping out of the tower into the brambles, he leaps into the thorny "arms" of the witch. The blinding brambles are the thorns that surround the rose of erotic love. His joyous vision is rapaciously snatched from him; the puerile vision had on high is punctured.

The prince plunges into an underworld of blindness and uncertainty and must find his way on his own, his rite of transition unassisted by male elders. Life transitions unattended by the midwifery of prior generations must be evolved *de novo*, each step uncertain, and the knowledge that is gained is only slowly trusted and integrated. A man or woman walking a lonely individuation path unassisted might, as Jung says, "fall into a black hole" at any time (Jung 1973, p. 623).

The prince's behavior toward Rapunzel is that of the "eternal youth" or *puer aeternus*. Like Hermes, the thief, he sneaks into the witch's tower, reprising the motif of the husband sneaking into the witch's garden. The prince relates to Rapunzel at night and weds her "high" in the tower – not grounded in parental support. He hopes to escape with her down a silken ladder without her godmother's knowledge. When this plan fails he hopes to make a run for it – like Eros escaping the hot oil of discovery. As an inner dilemma, his behavior illustrates an attempt to keep the psychic reality of relationship in shadow, out of dialogue and out of "contact with other interests" (Jung 1937, par. 131).

Because the prince cannot "see" any of this, he is brought down with a wound to his eyes. "Puer wounds always occur in specific images within specific stories, and more: they are local wounds to specific body-parts: Achilles' heel, Pelops's shoulder" (Hillman 1979, p. 102). The prince's blindness is reminiscent of that of Teiresias or Oedipus, signifying that the prince must acquire inward sight and recognize the role of the gods with whom he has been unconsciously dealing.

> [T]he puer takes its drive and goal literally unless there is reflection, which makes possible a metaphorical understanding of its drive and goal. By bearing witness as the receptive experiencer and imager of the spirit's actions, the soul can contain, nourish, and elaborate in fantasy the puer impulse, bring it sensuousness and depth, involve it in life's delusions, care for it for better or worse. Then the individual in whom these two components are marrying begins to carry with him his own reflective mirror and echo. He becomes aware of what his spiritual actions mean in terms of psyche. The spirit turned toward psyche, rather than deserting it for high places and cosmic love, finds ever further possibilities of seeing through the opacities and obfuscations in the valley. Sunlight enters the vale. (Ibid., p. 67)

In the searching and reflection induced by the prince's blindness, the puer impulse is grounded in inner sight.

Prior to reunion, Rapunzel lives in a desert place in misery and want with the twins she has borne. The desert suggests extremes of climate — dry and barren — none of the moisture of the witch's garden or of the feeling relationship with the prince. It also means that she has been "desert"-ed, abandoned, thrust out pregnant and alone. This is quite a "witch's brew" of initiation into independence, mothering, and nursing!

Alone, Rapunzel's Demetrian knowledge of vegetation and Hecatean skill in nursing come forward that she and her twins might survive.

Rapunzel brings together two worlds: the witch's virginal world of feminine resourcefulness and nursing with her mother's world of relatedness to the masculine, marriage, and childbirth. These "twins" live in Rapunzel's soul and are symbolized by the twins to whom she gives birth. Twins embody duality in unity, the tension of opposites. In her caring for the twins, Rapunzel nurses the tension of two worlds previously irreconcilable.

It may be that in the psychic background of a woman becoming pregnant and birthing a child, darker, more Hecatean/Demetrian energies make their presence felt. With Rapunzel's mother the pregnancy and birth "crossroads" brought forth the witch. So, too, with Rapunzel herself, her pregnancy and birthing bring forth the witch once more—banishing a woman's girlishness and puncturing a boyish husband's vision of joy.

In such circumstances many couples founder. New mothers with their children, like Rapunzel, live in a kind of desert, a mother/child domain, where the new mother must resurrect all that she has absorbed of the Hecatean/Demetrian energies of prior generations for the new family to survive.

The lover/husband may take a long time like the prince to become grounded in his new role. When erotic love in a cherished image is lost—through a change in the beloved, the end of an affair, or as in this instance, the woman becoming a mother, the "puer aeternus" male may "leap" into denial or flight. He may go "wandering," looking in a "womanizing" manner for his lost love, his anima image of Rapunzel, seeking this image with many partners. Sometimes this is a lifelong pattern. Sometimes, as with our couple, the respective bearing of burdens separately yet suffering together, can make reconnection possible. Rapunzel's salty tears, bitter yet moist, restore the prince's sight. The sharing of sufferings makes reunion on a more conscious level, where one can see more clearly, possible.

REFERENCES

Boer, C., trans. 1979. The Homeric hymn to Demeter. In *The Homeric Hymns*. Irving, Texas: Spring Publications.

DeVries, A. 1974. *Dictionary of Symbols and Imagery*. Amsterdam: North-Holland Publishing Co.

Farrer, C. R. 1987. Singing for life: the Mescalero Apache girls' puberty ceremony. In *Betwixt and Between*, L. C. Mahdi, S. Foster, and M. Little, eds. LaSalle, Ill.: Open Court.

Graves, R. 1960. *The Greek Myths*, vol. 1. Baltimore: Penguin Books.

Greene, L. 1984. *Astrology of Fate*. New York: Samuel Weiser.

Hillman, J. 1972. An essay on Pan. In *Pan and the Nightmare*, J. Hillman and W. H. Roscher. Zurich: Spring Publications.

_____. 1975. *Revisioning Psychology*. New York: Harper and Row.

_____. 1979. *Puer Papers*. Irving, Texas: Spring Publications.

Jong, E. 1981. *Witches*. New York: The New American Library.

Jung, C. G. 1926. Spirit and life. *CW* 8:319–337. Princeton, N.J.: Princeton University Press, 1960.

_____. 1937. Psychology and religion. *CW* 11:3–105. Princeton, N.J.: Princeton University Press, 1969.

_____. 1951. The psychology of the child archetype. *CW* 9i:151–181. Princeton, N.J.: Princeton University Press, 1959.

_____. 1957. Commentary on "The Secret of the Golden Flower." *CW* 13:1–56. Princeton, N.J.: Princeton University Press, 1967.

_____. 1973. *Letters*. Princeton, N.J.: Princeton University Press.

_____. 1977. *Speaking*. Princeton N.J.: Princeton University Press.

Kerenyi, K. 1977. *Eleusis: Archetypal Image of Mother and Daughter*. New York: Schocken Books.

_____. 1978. *Athene*. Murray Stein, trans. Zurich: Spring Publications.

_____. 1979. *Goddesses of Sun and Moon*. Murray Stein, trans. Irving, Texas: Spring Publications.

Klein, E. 1971. *A Comprehensive Etymological Dictionary of the English Language*. New York: Elsevier Scientific Publishing Co.

Kundera, M. 1984. *The Unbearable Lightness of Being*. M. H. Heim, trans. New York: Harper and Row.

Lincoln, B. 1981. *Emerging from the Chrysalis*. Cambridge, Mass.: Harvard University Press.

Manheim, R., trans. 1977. *Grimm's Tales for Young and Old*. Garden City, N.Y.: Doubleday.

Onians, R. B. 1953. *The Origins of European Thought*. Cambridge: Cambridge University Press.

Rose, J. 1972. *Herbs and Things*. New York: Grosset and Dunlap.

Stern, D. 1985. *The Interpersonal World of the Infant*. New York: Basic Books.

Tripp, E. 1970. *The Meridian Handbook of Classical Mythology*. New York: The New American Library.

Walker, B. 1983. *The Woman's Encyclopedia of Myths and Secrets*. San Francisco: Harper and Row.

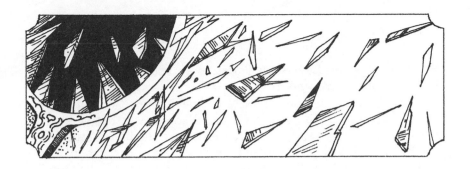

"The Snow Queen"
An Interpretation

Marilyn L. Matthews

The telling of stories, especially of fairy tales, has been a part of our cultural heritage for thousands of years. These tales give us examples of how to live our lives in accordance with the Self. Each tale shows a different facet of the Self in its many variations. There was a time when the oral tradition was the way people learned not only about their culture but also about themselves. Telling stories was not just for children, although children are most receptive. Stories were also for adults and the child within the adult.

When I am with an analysand listening to her story, I am also paying attention to the hints from my own unconscious. If a fairy tale comes to mind, I will wait a little while to see if it fits the analysand's struggle. While telling the story, I notice how she listens to the telling, whether she has the child's open mind. When the receptivity is there, as it often is with the right timing, there is no need for me to interpret the story. It is its own meaning. And the analysand, given the chance, will allow the tale and the imagery to do its own work.

The tale I have chosen is one which I have found useful for those women who have experienced psychic, physical, or emotional abandonment. Abandonment issues are quite prominent in all borderline, narcissistic, and histrionic character disorders.

Since many people have some variation of these traits, this story has value for many who hear it.

The fairy tale is about a girl's journey to find her lost play-mate, a little boy. Hers is not the usual heroic tale, but is about perseverance in spite of all odds. And about the inner "stuff" of her Being which helps her even though she know little about her truth. This is a story about heart, and the true spirit to be found in a girl who seeks and finds her own path.

The Snow Queen

The tale begins with hobgoblins who have made a mirror that "reflected everything that was good and beautiful in such a way that it dwindled almost to nothing but anything that was bad and ugly stood out very clearly and looked much worse" (Langs 1967, p. 76). These nasty little fellows were on their way to take the mirror up to God to reflect Him but were laughing so hard at their fantasies of the effect that they dropped the mirror. It broke into a million fragments. These fragments, if lodged in a person's eye would distort his vision, and if in his heart, turn it to ice.

In a large city, so crowded that there was no room for a garden, lived two poor children, Gerda and her friend, Kai. They lived with their parents and a grandmother, in two garrets very close together, sharing tiny roses in a window box. One evening while the snow was falling, the grandmother told the children a story about snow bees with the queen in their midst. Kai threatened to melt this queen if she ever came into the house. Later that evening, he thought he saw a snowflake enlarge into a beautiful pale lady.

One afternoon the following summer—at precisely five o'clock—Kai said that he'd gotten something in his eye, as well as feeling a prick in his heart. Two splinters from the broken mirror had entered his body. Soon his behavior changed. No longer did he want to play with Gerda, nor was he interested in the stories the grandmother told. Instead, he made fun of both of them and ran off to play with the other little boys.

On a winter evening, Kai tied his sled to the back of a large sled to have a fine ride. But the sled went too fast, and soon they were far away. It was the Snow Queen's sled; she stopped, wrapped him in her fur coat, and kissed him twice. Her kisses turned his heart into a lump of ice, and he forgot all about Gerda and the others. The Snow Queen took him to her ice palace far away to the north.

Gerda became very sad without her friend. She looked all over town for him, but no one knew where he was. Finally, because of her yearning, Gerda set out to find Kai. She went to the river and cast in her new red shoes, but the shoes only came back. Then she got into a boat and floated downstream until she reached the dwelling of an old woman, who had a very large garden. This woman wanted to keep Gerda with her so she combed the girl's hair, making her forget her quest. The old lady buried all her roses, for she knew that if Gerda saw a rose she would remember the window-box roses of her home and her search for Kai. For a long time Gerda was content, although she sensed there was one flower missing in the garden. One day, while looking at the old woman's hat on which roses were painted, she remembered Kai and her search to find him. She left the garden in her bare feet and walked out into late fall with snow on the ground.

She met a crow, who told her about the princess's recent marriage. This princess, it seems, was very intelligent and wanted to marry a man who was her equal. Although many suitors came, they were all too impressed with the princess's wealth and outward trappings. Then a poor common youth came, not to woo her, but to find out if she was really as smart as she had said. He was not awed by all the gold and ceremony and was able to converse with the princess; he won her hand in marriage.

When Gerda heard this story, she immediately thought it was Kai and wanted to see him right then. The crow arranged the meeting, and the prince, who was not Kai, and princess, feeling sorry for her, made her welcome. They arranged for a golden coach, servants to accompany her, and fine clothes to send her on her way. In the forest the party was attacked by robbers and all the servants killed. Only through the intervention of the robber maiden—the daughter of the fierce old robber mother—was Gerda saved. This robber maiden took Gerda home where she scared Gerda with her sadistic behavior toward her captive animals. However, the maid was also touched by Gerda's plight, and she freed the reindeer to carry Gerda to the far north.

On the journey, they stopped at an old Laplander woman's home, and she sent them on to an old Finnish woman's house, farther north. This old woman recognized Gerda's innate strength and sent her off with bare feet and hands to the Snow Queen's palace.

Once there, only Gerda's strength of heart and spirit carried her on. Once she saw Kai—who was trying to form the word "Love" so that he could gain his freedom—she fell on his neck, crying. Her tears melted the ice in his heart so he, too, began to cry, and the splinters floated out of his eyes. They celebrated each other, and while they slept, the word "Love" was formed by the ice shards. As they traveled back home and entered the city, they discovered they had grown up.

Fairy tales often personify functions in humanity's search for wholeness. In our present day, the power of the dark side has distorted man's ability to see himself. In my interpretation of this tale about the Snow Queen, I will limit myself to those issues that pertain to the distortions of abandonment—issues present in many women in a patriarchal culture which devalues the feminine—although this elaboration is not the only possibility.

Just as in a dream, the beginning sets the tone for the rest of the story. The first elements to appear are the hobgoblins, who were considered evil and wicked. These ugly little gnomelike creatures were associated with dwarves and goblins. Hobgoblins were viewed as personifications of the hidden forces of nature; in women's dreams they often represent the devilish or stunted side of the Father-Spirit image (de Vries 1976).

These hobgoblins have made a mirror that distorts all it reflects. Anything that is good and beautiful is turned bad and ugly. The abandoned woman has introjected a distorted mirror. Her heart has been pierced by a shard, just as Kai's was. Consequently, in therapy, any mirroring by the therapist is received in a distorted way. Women with abandonment fears have difficulty reflecting on their behavior, as well as on their dreams. They forget what they are like from mood to mood, and session to session. If we examine the mirror in this story, we see, in its magnification of faults, something quite similar to the internal critical voices in many women. In this story, Gerda has all that she needs for her wholeness inside of her. But, as with many women, the conscious connection to her own beauty has been lost or distorted by external forces. The abandoned woman is disconnected from her own potential, her own source, by these distortions and negative inflations. When the mirror shatters, the journey begins, and so also the possibility for healing.

The setting of the tale, in an overcrowded city, indicates a loss of connection to nature in the growing industrialization of society. Men and women stripped of their mythological roots, which might have helped them make sacred their existence and thus prevent hubris, now face a reflection of both inflation and disharmony.

The rose plants – which connect the homes of the boy and girl – are a symbol of the female generative principles of love, youth, and spring. The rose can also represent a union of opposites with the mystical center at the heart. For Jung, the rose was a wholeness symbol of the Self, the balance between the conscious and the unconscious. The abandoned woman has no connection to her true Self, nor does she have a good relationship to her animus. This tale then shows one possibility for a woman to gain access not only to the *coniunctio*, represented by the two children, Gerda and Kai, but also to find the path to her true Self, through the journey itself.

The only other character mentioned with any force in the beginning of the tale is the old grandmother. Thus we see a foursome made up of three feminine elements and one masculine: the old grandmother in her beneficent aspect; the Snow Queen with all her icy, cold, hard brilliance; the little girl, Gerda, unproven in her innocence; and the little boy, Kai, who dares to pit himself against the dark aspect of this feminine power. Although there are various ways to interpret any fairy tale, the triumvirate of the feminine goddess – the old one, the queen, and the maid – and the fact that it is the little girl who must make the heroic journey suggests that this tale is primarily about woman's individuation. The fact that in this story the Snow Queen stands in for the mother in the triumvirate resonates with the plight of the abandoned female. Many of these women see their mothers as cold, hard, and icy. If we are interpreting this tale psychologically, then Gerda may represent the childlike ego of the abandoned woman, for many of these women, although physically mature, remain psychologically childlike. The grandmother represents the wise old woman, the wisdom of the earth, the deepest feminine core. The woman who has been abandoned has this wisdom inside her as part of her strength, but as a child, she has not yet utilized it. Kai represents a youthful animus figure, not yet mature, filled with fun and braggadocio. He does not come to the girl as hero or rescuer. Rather, he comes as playmate and equal.

The very next summer, after Kai has had his first glimpse of his fate, at precisely five o'clock in the afternoon, he is invaded by the fragments of the shattered mirror. The connection between the mirror's distortions and the Snow Queen can be seen in the time of day that Kai is invaded by the splinters. The number five is a number of the Great Goddess and can have significance in initiation. Five is also a number which "corresponds to the indistinguishability of quaternity and unity" (Jung 1951, par. 351 n. 10).

Following this incident the boy loses all respect and compassion for the little girl, Gerda. He ridicules and criticizes the feminine in all its aspects, including friendship and nature. He goes off to play with his boy friends in activities that exclude the girl/woman. In one of the versions of this tale, the emphasis is on the boy's development of math and reason, to the point that ridicule and imitation of others become the rule. The more the boy chooses these pursuits, the less open he is to his heart and feelings. The ridiculing and degrading of the feminine is part and parcel of the abandoned woman's own difficulty. Indeed, this is how the negative mother complex is complicated by animus possession.

In the next part of the story, the boy gets carried off by the Snow Queen who kisses him twice but no more because she herself is aware that the third kiss would kill him. These two kisses, however, make him forget Gerda and the grandmother. He is now totally in the power of the Snow Queen and lives with her in her palace. The Snow Queen as icy mother steals the girl's animus and uses it for herself. This rings true for many women in dysfunctional families. Whenever the girl strives for independence, her mother takes over her spirit, making it difficult for the girl to think. For example, a woman remembered as a child being frustrated with arithmetic. Her mother had bragged about how well she had been able to do her sums and logic problems. Around this mother, the daughter was unable to use her natural ability to think. In the dysfunctional family, the daughter complies with the mother's theft of her spirit. The normal roles of mirroring are reversed; instead of the mother mirroring the daughter, the daughter has to be available to her mother, to soothe her, make her happy, to "fix" her and make mother feel better about herself. It rarely works; the more the daughter gives of herself, the more the mother criticizes her.

The rest of the story of "The Snow Queen" details the ways in which the girl searches for her lost friend, Kai. It is a heroic journey, but done in a feminine rather than a masculine way. This is what the abandoned woman must do: she must reclaim the lost masculine from the grip of the Ice Mother. It is not just a matter of getting in touch with or relating to her animus, although that is important. These women are often so thoroughly caught in a negative animus situation that there is minimal energy left, and very little sense of self-worth. They must regain the lost abandoned child and with that redemption, find their own true Self.

In one version of the story, Gerda throws her new red shoes into the river and, adrift in a rowboat, floats down the stream for miles. In order to begin looking for the missing boy, she must sacrifice her newly acquired standpoint. Red shoes suggest several possibilities among which are courage, emotions, sexuality, and love, all of which are problem areas for the abandoned female. Thus, a woman trying to regain touch with this lost creativity, this frozen energy, must be willing to give up certain sentiments about love and to take more seriously certain emotional processes, rather than discarding or trivializing them. Gerda's journey begins, then, with a willing loss of her emotional standpoint, a willingness to float down the river and be carried by the process. The willingness to float with the process is sometimes a difficult experience for the woman whose willfullness and need to control out of fear is evident.

Gerda's first stop is with an old woman who has a house with a garden and cherry orchard. The old woman combs the girl's hair and Gerda forgets her task. Cherries are a fruit of Ceres (Demeter). The comb is associated with the Sirens, as an enticement to entanglement. The old woman, although not negative, puts all the roses in her garden underground (for the rose might remind Gerda not only of her task, but also of her connection to Kai and her Self). This image might be likened to a woman's early stage of animus development when she is still caught in the maternal uroboros. The old maternal order does not want an equal partner but only a son/lover. The old woman has no old man to share her life; instead she wants the girl to keep her company. Perhaps she even wants, like the hysterogenic and/or borderline mother, to use Gerda's youthful energy to fill her emptiness. Empty, because she, too, was not seen and valued. The ability to see, as Alice Miller (1984) observes, has been sadly disavowed. Childrearing practices manipulate and disavow real feelings. The child learns –

as has her mother and father before her—to pretend. And the emptiness begins.

This early maternal stage is reflected in the story of Demeter and Persephone when the maid lives in harmony with mother in uroboric containment. To grow up, Gerda must accept responsibility for her own relationship to her creative energy.

As time goes by, Gerda becomes aware that one flower is missing from the garden. However, she does not remember which one until she sees the roses painted on the old woman's hat. That the roses were there implies an incompleteness to this matriarchal scheme. The man is missing or immature. His presence as an equal part of the old woman's life is not defined. Hats often represent thoughts. The girl begins to think and remembers her goal. She gets free from the old woman's spell when she begins to think consciously and to remember her love.

In the original story, the other flowers in the garden each have their own story, but the girl must pay attention to her own. That is, she must choose to limit her concern for others in order to consciously integrate the masculine. Rather similar are the directions given Psyche in her last task (see the tale of Amor and Psyche in *The Golden Ass* by Apuleius), when she is warned not to reach out to all the pitiable people who want her help or she will be lost. If Gerda allows herself to become scattered by listening to all the other flowers' tales, she will lose her focus of reconnecting to Kai. The girl is now beginning to take some steps in freeing herself from the domination of the unconscious.

It seems to me that the first part of Gerda's journey is similar to what must happen in the treatment of a woman caught in the negative animus/negative mother complex. There must be a willingness to give up a certain kind of ego standpoint and "go with the flow." It is difficult for a woman possessed by a driving animus to allow an awareness of unconscious or semiconscious fantasies because this flow often leads to a regression. This regressed state, a "mothered" state, is one in which she can experience in a different way the merger/fusion so important for the development of her self-esteem. When she can allow herself to experience this regression and its inherent dependency, she can then find acceptance for her own true Self. Eventually her own inner needs to grow up, to move on, come into her awareness. It is then that this woman begins to think in a different way than when she first came into analysis. She becomes aware of herself thinking. It is her own active process. She is no longer under the domination of the internal critical voices. She experiences herself as having power. Although this power is not yet strong, it is a beginning, a step forward to experience herself as an active participant, not just the passive victim of circumstances.

When Gerda comes out of the garden, it is no longer summer. Her feet are bare yet she continues to walk, even in the snow. Gerda's feet walk directly on the earth. The foot often symbolizes phallic, generative power, but Gerda's feet are on the ground, very much in touch with the maternal. Her journey leads into the darkness of winter – psychologically an emotional wasteland – yet there is a strength from this standpoint on the earth which enables her to continue. This barefoot winter's trek reminds me of Inanna's trip to the underworld where she must strip naked, be killed, and hung on a peg to rot. The symbol of the peg and the hanging on it becomes the woman's connection to her own yang principle (Perera 1981). This new yang energy is different from just going out and doing something. It is more like having a firm backbone that allows the woman to feel supported in her tasks. In order to reach this level of grounding, the woman must feel her suffering deeply yet continue despite the difficulties. The strength to go on seems to be related to something deeply feminine, a source of power that can be found through the openness to suffering. It is particularly important for the abandoned woman to discover this truth as she frequently hides her own strength from herself and from others.

As she continues her journey, Gerda meets a crow who tells her the story of the clever princess's recent marriage. This little interjected story would seem unrelated except for the theme. The princess, an intelligent woman, wants to marry only that man who can speak for himself. She is not willing to settle for anyone who stands around looking distinguished. The men who come on the first two days after the princess announces her intent to marry are too impressed with her wealth. They could not see past the overweening pride of the servants dressed in gold and silver. These suitors, as well as the falsely proud servants, are a part of the collective animus. A woman identified with the animus – as many women are in our current patriarchal culture whose only choice is that of identifying with the aggressor – knows only the collective truths and mouths them like an echo. There is, then, an associated arrogance in these women that impedes any further attempts at relating.

That the princess wants a mate who can speak up for himself implies that her power is real and needs equal and opposite strength for a satisfactory marriage. Because the abandoned woman has been raised to disbelieve her own competence, she sees herself as passive. Many women are taught to hide both strength and intelligence in order not to frighten off a marriage-able man. Their strength and activity remain hidden from them, whereas in this vignette, the princess knows her own intelligence and values herself enough to want a mate of equal ability. The best possible marriage would be one in which neither element dominates, yet each has its own strength, so that the resultant union is more that just the sum of its parts. Thus, a woman struggling with animus development must also value herself as woman and be able to take a stand vis-à-vis the collective. For her to have a satisfactory relationship to the animus, she must be able to see when it is voicing irrelevant facts as well as when she is caught up in its grandiosity.

The youth who wins the princess's hand is not overawed by the grandeur of her surroundings. He has a confidence that allows him to see reality. He tells her he has not come to woo her but to see if she really is as clever and intelligent as she has said. Many women choose a different option. More often than not they are attracted to a man whose narcissistic traits are obvious. This choice, I believe, reflects the woman's own narcisisstic deficits. However, choosing such a man could also hold a hidden *telos*. For the abandoned woman has become quite adept at living a false Self. She needs to reconnect to her own truth. But because she has lived with such devaluation of the feminine, her relationship with mother and, indeed, females in general is likely to be more in the shadow. Jung says that when a woman has not made some headway with her own shadow elements, the animus takes on the numinosity of the Self (1954, par. 342).

This part of the fairy tale shows a different option of how a marriage could be. The princess values her intelligence and does not try to hide it (in contrast to the many women who try to convince themselves and others that they have no strength or intelligence). The youth who comes to see the princess does so on his own feet. He is not confounded by external appearances nor does he require that the princess mirror him. He comes to see her truth, not to woo her, but to discover whether or not her claims are real. Each brings along a sense of connection to the Self, an intrinsic sense of self-esteem and self-worth. Neither of them is affected by external appearances; each sees the reality of the other. This vignette shows a different outcome for male/female interaction than does either of the myths from the old patriarchal pattern (see the Book of Tobit in the Apocryphal Old Testament and the story of Myrrha in Zabriskie (1982)) or the even older matriarchal ways (Demeter and Persephone). This is a marriage of equals.

Gerda, with the help of the crow, gets into the palace and, although she does not find Kai, elicits the sympathetic help of this royal couple. The crow, as messenger of Apollo, could signify a way of seeing from a distance, a clear vision of the future. However, the crow is also associated with the Great Goddess and as such may indicate in this tale some of the aspects of the female shadow (not necessarily bad) – the intuitive and thinking aspects – which need to become integrated. When shadow aspects are integrated, the relationship with the animus will also improve and thus allow the girl child, whose presence is a prominent part of the abandoned woman, to continue her growth.

In the next part of the story, Gerda is robbed of all the finery given her by the royal couple. On her way through the dark forest, robbers come and kill the servants. The robber mother wants to eat Gerda but the robber daughter intervenes. To psychologize this part of the tale, the girl's ego position is inflated – the fine clothing, gold carriage, and several servants. The split-off feminine – the parts of shadow represented by the robber mother and daughter – is envious and retaliates by again reducing the girl to her previous state. As Karen Horney (1934) states in her essay "Overvaluation of Love," there is often a bitter hatred and envy in the mother/daughter relationship. Unless those negative feelings are made conscious and worked through, they continue to undermine the woman's relationships with both women and men.

The robber mother is described as having a beard and large bushy eyebrows. A bearded woman is often a witch or at least represents a strongly phallic woman. These aspects are parts of the negative mother complex. The negativity is evoked when the woman begins to take some positive steps toward using her own power, her own active assertiveness. The split-off, dark aspects of the feminine become active and attempt to prevent the woman's growth. The attacks of the negative animus (in cahoots with the negative mother, being, in fact, her henchman) try to rob the woman of her goodness, her treasures. She must learn, as Castillejo (1973) points out, to question the internal voices and take a strong stand against the attacks. The emergence of the robber maiden who bites her own mother's ear in order to protect Gerda is significant. This robber girl is sadistic. She tortures the animals she imprisons. When a woman becomes aware of and acknowledges her own sadism, her own desire to control, she stands a much greater chance of withstanding the criticism of the negative animus attacks.

The last leg of Gerda's journey holds the most significance. In it we see the hidden truth: that she has all she needs inside her, in her heart. The reindeer takes Gerda first to the house of the Lapp woman, then on to the house of the Finnish woman. This latter is a woman of power. As the reindeer pleads the girl's cause, he gets a strange answer from this powerful old woman. She says: "I can't give her any more power than she already has! Don't you see how men and animals must serve her; how else could she have come so far, walking on her bare feet? But she must never learn of her power; it is in her heart, for she is a sweet and innocent child" (Anderson 1974, p. 257). The old woman knows the power of the heart will overcome all obstacles.

The reindeer, carrying out the old woman's instructions, takes Gerda to the entrance of the Snow Queen's palace where he leaves her. In her haste she has left behind her mittens and boots. So she is again exposed to the elements with no protection except her own resources. When the Snow Queen's guard attacks, she prays and her own breath becomes the angels of her protection. Breath and spirit are often associated – e.g. *pneuma* (Greek) and *ruach* (Hebrew). It is often the case that when we have our backs against the wall, when the situation seems the blackest, some power helps us, especially if we open ourselves to its presence. Thus, Gerda comes to the Snow Queen's palace with the most powerful force one can imagine: the truth of her loving spirit.

In the seventh tale, we are brought back to Kai, who has been living in the cold barrenness of this icy palace. In the center of this palace is a frozen lake – the Mirror of Reason--on which sits the Snow Queen's throne. Kai is there playing with pieces of ice, trying to arrange them into a word he cannot quite remember. The Snow Queen has promised that he will become his own master if he can spell this word. In the original story the word is *eternity*. In one of the variations, the word is *love*. In either case, Kai is too caught in the numbness of the power of the Snow Queen to be able to spell the unbinding word.

Now what situations from life does this bring to mind? Many times women get caught in the prison of helpless, hopeless victim/ martyr in which there is nothing they can do but suffer. And it is not even good suffering! There is perseveration not eternity, hatred and self-pity not love. The animus, frozen in the negative mother reasoning, is without playfulness or compassion.

The only way out for Gerda and Kai is through Gerda's healthy tears which melt the ice in Kai's heart. He then can start to cry and thus float the ice splinters out of his eyes. The tears here are very important. Psychologically different from the neurotic tears of the woman caught in the perpetuation of her own abandonment, these tears are the true grief of a loss that is felt deep in her gut. When Gerda sees just how distant and unavailable Kai has become at the hands of the Ice Mother, she feels the deepest grief and compassion. It is the tears of this depth of suffering that wash away the distortions preventing true vision. The abandoned woman, when she has reached this point, does not feel self-pity, but rather recognizes her participation in her own self-abandonment.

After the tears have flowed and the ice has melted, the two young people laugh and dance and sing together until they finally sleep on the ice. When we struggle for consciousness, the collective unconscious responds to our efforts; it gives us something back. In this case, while the children sleep, the word is formed that gives Kai his freedom. The boy and girl are now freed from the grip of the Snow Queen; the *coniunctio* has become reality. When they return home, they find that they have grown up. Yet they remain children at heart.

The way to redeem the soulmate, the creativity frozen in the negative mother, is through the essence of love. I prefer to use the word *soulmate* for the inner masculine because, like Irene Castillejo, I have listened to many women whose souls are feminine. When the woman can move through the difficulties of the dark feminine – the envious hatred and bitter cynicism of betrayal – she finds love. This process is an active struggle for the woman, and in the end her genuine tears cleanse her soul and free it from negativity.

REFERENCES

Anderson, Hans Christian. 1974. The snow queen. In *The Complete Fairy Tales and Stories*, E. C. Haugaard, trans. Garden City, N.Y.: Doubleday and Company.

Apuleius. *The Golden Ass*. William Adlington, trans. Harry C. Schnur, ed. New York: Collier Books, 1962.

Castillejo, Irene. 1973. *Knowing Woman*. New York: Harper and Row.

de Vries, Ad. 1976. *Dictionary of Symbols and Imagery* Amsterdam: North-Holland Publishing Company.

Horney, Karen. 1934. The overvaluation of love. In *Feminine Psychology*, Harold Kelman, ed. New York: W. W. Norton Co., 1967.

Jung, C. G. 1951. *Aion. Collected Works*, vol. 9ii. Princeton, N.J.: Princeton University Press, 1970.

———. 1954. The philosophical tree. *Collected Works* 13:251–349. Princeton, N.J.: Princeton University Press, 1970.

Langs, Andrew, ed. 1967. *The Pink Fairy Book*. New York: Dover Publications, Inc. (Originally published, 1897.)

Miller, Alice. 1984. *Thou Shalt Not Be Aware*. Hildegarde and Hunter Hannum, trans. New York: Farrar, Straus, Giroux.

Perera, Sylvia Brinton. 1981. *Descent to the Goddess*. Toronto: Inner City Books.

Zabriskie, Beverly. 1982. Incest and myrrh: father-daughter sex in therapy. *Quadrant* (Fall 1982): 5–24.

"Snow White," "Cinderella," and Dracula
When the Ferris Wheel Stops*

Ronald T. Curran

Rather than offering new interpretations of popular fairy tales in this essay, I will discuss the developmental implications of *Dracula*, "Snow White," and "Cinderella" as these stories appear in a big dream of "Karen," a ten-year-old girl. Her dream "uses" fairy tales to explore developmental issues surfacing as she moves from childhood to adolescence. In the dream she rides on a ferris wheel at the top of which she feels omnipotent. "It is like you are flying," she says, "a feeling of greatness and that I can do almost everything." But Dracula interrupts this moment of inflation, stops the ferris wheel, and Karen jumps, blacks out, and finds herself first in the story of "Snow White" and then in "Cinderella."

Her encounter with Dracula exposes problems in the formation of sexual identity and separation from parental complexes. "Snow White" and "Cinderella" elaborate these issues as well as introduce others like narcissism and sibling rivalry as Karen

*I wish to thank Lionel Corbett, Murray Stein, Pauline Napier, and Cleon Cornes for their comments on this manuscript. Dr. Corbett's remarks, in particular, guided me in balancing my more optimistic developmental interpretation with the darker, objective implications of Karen's dream. Any errors I made in using their commentary in this paper are entirely my own. My gratitude extends also to Stanton Marlan, director of the C. G. Jung Educational Center of Pittsburgh, whose seminar in dream interpretation helped to develop my understanding of this method of analysis.

moves from latency toward independence, autonomy, and mature sexuality. As in all children's dreams, the question of whether these issues are Karen's, her parents', or collective ones cannot be resolved easily. But analyzing how these fairy tales function in her dream gives us a chance to observe how they personify conflicts characteristic of a specific child's movement into adolescence.

Their appearance in Karen's dream reinforces the archetypal nature of these conflicts. How they represent the role of the unconscious as they personify gender conflict argues that traditional fairy tales do not determine such roles. Instead, as Karen's dream reveals, they provide images and patterns which generate a useful tension between the archetypal and cultural aspects of the tales. That tension facilitates unique personality style. Fairy tales do not, as feminist critics have argued, function inherently as regressive cultural prescriptions for anachronistic gender roles.

Speaking of Jung's theory of archetypes in relation to fairy tales in particular, von Franz sees an archetype as "a special psychic impulse, producing its effect like a single ray of radiation, and at the same time a whole magnetic field expanding in all directions" (1970, p. 2). She sees the archetypal content of fairy tales as "not only an 'elementary thought' but also an elementary poetical image and fantasy, and an elementary emotion, and even an elementary impulse towards some typical action. So we add to it," she continues, "a whole sub-structure of feeling, emotion, fantasy, and action" (ibid., p. 6). For her, "an archetypal image is not only a thought-pattern. . .it is also an emotional experience – the emotional experience of an individual. Only if it has an emotional and feeling value for an individual is it alive and meaningful" (ibid., p. 7).

In Karen's dream these aspects of its archetypal content are self-evident. But this is especially true in the unique way that this content creates an ambivalent tension toward her taking "some typical action." The archetypal content of Karen's dream reflects the elementary thoughts, poetical images, fantasies, and emotions and impulses toward typical actions; it adds a whole substructure of feeling, emotion, fantasy, and action in its affective dimension. Karen's dream goes as follows:

> *I'm on a ferris wheel by myself in one of the booths on it. There are other people on it, too. Suddenly the ferris wheel stops and Dracula starts climbing up the ferris wheel to where I am. (I am on the very top.)*

So I jump out and black out. Then when I wake up the seven dwarfs are looking at me. I am in the casket that the dwarfs built for Snow White when they thought that she was dead, but it is like a wooden bed almost. Then when they see I have woken up, they cheer and start dancing around me in a circle. I ask the oldest one, the one who is more normal and human, where I am. And he says: "Why, Snow White, don't you know us?" I look at myself and see that I look like Snow White. I go along with the dwarfs until the end of the story, then I black out. I lose consciousness. The whole story in unfolding. It is going extra fast and is blurry, until the prince is marrying Snow White. Then it ends and blacks out. I black out right after I marry the prince.

Then I black out again and find myself as Cinderella on the night of the ball, just when the fairy godmother is changing me into the beautiful ball dress. So I come to the ball and go along with everything until the end, and then I black out again. I do everything that Cinderella does – the prince comes to the house. I try on the slipper, etc. I can see all of the action because I am moving through it all. But it goes by quickly like the story of Snow White did. I black out after I marry the prince.

This time I find myself back with the dwarfs, and they are taking me to the mines where they work, and I see diamonds, rubies, sapphires, and gold and silver and other gems piled up in barrels and heaps and many are still on the walls. The dwarfs are hiding down in the mine as people are marching above the mine. I hear their drums, and I catch a glimpse of them. Some are in Civil War uniforms, some from the Revolutionary War; some are knights like the ones in fairy tales. With an extra loud crack the mine collapses on the dwarfs and me, but I escape and find myself in my own bed.

The feeling dimension to Karen's experience in the dream is indicated by the dream ego. She associates that the ferris wheel is in "a lone place," an area that is "barren and rocky," "desertlike." The representation of psyche here is dry, arid, and isolated from "the rest of the park." The other rides one can take in life cannot at this point be seen very clearly. The psychic space personifies her feelings of sadness, "like a person who had cried so much that they didn't have any more tears left." But not all the water has disappeared; there are "water holes," oases on this desert feeling that contains the possibility of a precondition for renewal.

The tension created by the paradox of Karen's inflation and sadness nicely describes the affect at this developmental juncture. It reflects the bittersweet feeling of being on the borderline, of being at the top end of one phase of childhood and at the beginning of another, adolescence. The developmental tasks of the initial period of childhood have been mastered, and there is a feeling of exhilaration and inflation. But the challenges of the next phase intrude and make their threatening demands. Karen's images resonate with the playful sense of being at the amusement park on the sand of a riverless desert where the water still exists but does not flow. While these images embody these feeling-state tensions, Dracula appears.

Vulnerably caught up in the conflicts at this time and while she is in transition. Karen must face the threat of his awesome power. Her leap into space and blacking out provide a phenomenological definition of what Karen must experience as extreme anxiety; her frequent blackouts indicate the traumatic nature of the dream ego's feeling state. Karen's psyche is caught in what Edinger called "the process of alternation between ego-Self union and ego-Self separation," which he says "seems to occur repeatedly throughout the life of the individual both in childhood and in maturity" (1973, p. 5). The desert images the feeling of alienation which accompanies inflation. As the ego differentiates in the first half of life, it also loses touch with the inner world, with Self, and that is in part the desert experience we see in Karen's dream.

The ferris wheel stops at this stage of Karen's development. "It stopped," she said, "because Dracula stopped it. He stopped it just to get at me!"[1] Bram Stoker's *Dracula* is the first of the three archetypal stories which symbolize her experience of sexual and emotional development and put it into narrative form. Dracula helps Karen to personify the threat that she feels. The ferris wheel-mandala symbol of wholeness and the eternal circular process of life itself stops when he appears. Stoker's story of the blood-drinking vampire-count provides both a figure and a story which allow Karen to image her inflation, her sense of being a

---

[1]Leonard's comments on Dracula in her chapter, "The Demon Lover" (1987), apply as well to how this archetypal figure functions in Karen's psychic life:

> The story of Dracula tells a mythic truth. Its characters are symbols of human experience; its actions are our actions. We have within ourselves all these figures, struggling with the forces of good and evil, the ultimate conflict of opposites at war in human existence. As such, Dracula, the Demon Lover in the psyche, is the epitome of the ultimate obstacle on the way to the wedding. (Leonard 1987, p. 88)

puella aeterna. Dracula's sexual initiation (the first bite) carries Karen's anxieties about adolescent sexuality. When Dracula appears, time and movement through space stop, and the image of wholeness is left behind momentarily. Karen's dream ego jumps out of her booth at the top of the ferris wheel and blacks out.

Dracula is the negative animus figure in Karen's dream, one which carries a considerable projection of the shadow.[2] He represents qualities defined by culture as inappropriate to the sexual identity of the ego. These are repressed into the unconscious and appear in the dream life personified by a figure of the contrasexual other. He appears at a critical developmental juncture, puberty, the gateway to adolescence. Dracula's archetypal character helps to form a link between Karen's own and the collective experience; it provides a container for a complex constellation of developmental issues. His aristocratic style, social elegance, and verbal polish characterize a persona behind which he masks his vulnerability. He is like Hermes in his aspect of god of eloquence, social ease, cunning, and perjury. Omnipotent in his mountaintop castle, the symbol of his inflation, isolation, and power, Dracula presents a perverse image of the *puer aeternus* insofar as his egotism fuels his quest for immortality. For the ultimate narcissistic wish of the *puer* is to live forever, to be forever young. As an image of the puer at a later stage of development, Dracula provides a portrait far removed from the experience of a ten-year-old.

Further, Leonard asserts, "Dracula represents our own will to power—though to gain his power we must give up our will to his. Thus ultimately those who become his victims do not resist him" (ibid., p. 89). Later she quotes Richard Geer, director of the stage version by Richard Sharp: "Dracula is the essence of evil's awesome attraction. We admire him and are horrified by our admiration of this elegant symbol of temptation" (ibid.).

[2] I would like to qualify my use of the Jungian concept of the animus in this paper. It is well known that Jung's definition of it was influenced considerably by the cultural perceptions of gender in late Victorian society. See, for example, Naomi Goldenberg, "A Feminist Critique of Jung" (1976); Irene Claremont de Castillejo, *Knowing Women: A Feminine Psychology* (1973); and Mary Ann Mattoon and Jennette Jones, "Is the Animus Obsolete?" (1987). My use of animus in this paper follows that of Emma Jung in *Animus and Anima* (1969). The animus has any number of manifestations both negative and positive in character. Further, negative manifestations of the animus, like Dracula in Karen's dream, reflect the need to develop particular aspects of the woman's masculine side, to make conscious, integrate, and thus release the positive energy they contain.

He prefigures the long-term consequences of ego inflation in his emotional immaturity and exploitative style.

Dracula comes after Karen on many levels. At this one he is as much a mirror as he is a monster. He carries the projection of Karen's *puella aeterna*, her eternal girl. Karen flees from a frightening image of the future as much as she does from one that is an immediate threat in the present. Not to cross the developmental border is to get caught up in the illusion, of which the inflation is the symptom, that time can be stopped. The living deadness of that condition requires the blood of others to sustain the fiction of being alive.

Karen would notice that Dracula is more a threat to women and children than to men. Jonathan Harker, the English solicitor who visits the count, is set upon unsuccessfully by three phantom women, and later he is weak and sick from a strange wound in his throat. But he is never in the same danger as Lucy Westenra. Unlike the death of Lucy, the betrothed friend of his own fiancée, Mina Murray, Harker's is never imminent. The attack on the betrothed indicates that the fear Dracula embodies is felt primarily by virgins about to be married and initiated into sexuality. Thus the idea of being possessed, having one's blood sucked out, being one of the "phantom" women of Dracula seems a dominant one in the text. It marks a transformation after sexual initiation which itself involves a "death" and then a life of bloodsucking. Karen responded to this also in her association when she said, "I feared that he would suck my blood, and then I would have to go around sucking other people's blood." After the phallic bite women become like men, like Dracula. The bite not only drains; it infects. For, thus contaminated, the women in turn corrupt innocence. As an animus figure which carries the projection of the feminine shadow, Dracula also represents the dark side of sexuality. He personifies its parasitic and enslaving aspects, and he embodies the wish that exploitative erotic renewal can prolong life.

To be his "bride," then, involves a transformation; first there is a "death," and then a rebirth into a life of bloodsucking. In psychological terms, identification with the masculine turns the woman into a Dracula figure herself. In a way this attitude, in part a cultural one, is predictable in this 1897 novel because the Victorian repression of sexuality surfaces in this fantasy example of the return of the repressed in the world of the imagination. Its resurfacing in Karen's dream, however, suggests that it may have an archetypal dimension as well. The conclusion of the novel shows the intensity of the repression in the desire to kill Count Dracula, to kill the shadow of the dark side of love. To be rid of the potential host-parasite relation which enslaves and drains eros. But the bipolar aspect of the archetype of sexuality which Dracula also personifies reflects the positive feeling of power, nourishment, and vitality in sexual awakening and relationship. In Stoker's text it is a power being seen in its negative aspect and rejected.

Dracula also suggests the dark side of Hecate, the earth goddess who, like Demeter, looked after the fertility of the ground. Not the Hecate who bestows wealth and success, good luck and advice in her aspect as the goddess of plenty, but the one who is an infernal deity, snakelike and terrible, queen of ghosts and mistress of black magic. Both she and Dracula, like animus and anima, represent the female and male shadow sides of sexuality, goddess and god of border crossings like those between virginity and sexual experience. Dracula, in particular, represents the archetype of love as possession, as soul theft. Indeed, he who becomes engaged and dares to cross the border, either the one from virginity to sexual experience or the one from self to other, meets up with Hecate, goddess of roads, of border areas, and with Count Dracula as well.

But the figure of Dracula in Karen's dream has its objective dimension in Karen's experience of her family. The intense and potentially destructive envy experienced both by Snow White and Cinderella suggests that Karen may experience a similar emotion from her mother, father, or siblings. Negative relationships with any of these people could produce a destructive figure like Dracula. If we focus on the mother because of the threatening maternal figures in the two fairy tales, we see that her thoughts in regard to Karen are negative ("she hates me because I'm prettier than her") and somewhat disguised ("you can never really see her because her hood is over her head"). Is the mother jealous because of the father's relation with Karen? Is she jealous because Karen has qualities she (the mother) covets but lacks herself?

Do both parents "fight" for possession of Karen's primary allegiance? Does someone in the family want to fight with or destroy anything good in the child's psyche? (Recall that the count has no image in the mirror, and that absence may indicate how envy from whatever source in the family could inhibit or even destroy Karen's imagination or her relation to her inner life.) Is Karen's "war" necessary for her to develop independence from the negative introject (Dracula/parent or sibling) which attacks her? Does a complex of either or both parents lead to the setting of unduly high expectations which Karen cannot fulfill? ("They are all kind men. I get the impression that they are under a spell or they wouldn't do this.") Is this why the mine collapses? ("There's too much pressure on top.") Dracula also could suggest sibling rivalry which is a major area of conflict in "Cinderella." All of these possibilities and doubtless others would have to be considered in long-term work with Karen as well as the sexual connotations which I have developed in my amplification of Dracula.

As I mentioned, Karen's pursuit by Dracula leads to her escape by literally falling into two fairy tales, "Snow White" and "Cinderella." Identification and projection help her to symbolize her experience through these narratives, to make psychological sense of events. The developmental issues and conflicts surfacing at puberty are located by Karen's psyche in the symbolic worlds of these fantasy texts.

James Hillman points out in *Loose Ends* that "one integrates life as story because one has stories in the back of the mind (unconscious) as containers for organizing events into meaningful experiences. The stories are means," he adds, "of telling oneself into events that might not otherwise make psychological sense at all" (Hillman 1975, p. 1). "Having had stories built in with childhood," he continues, "a person is usually in better relation with the pathologized material of obscene, grotesque or cruel images which appear spontaneously in dream and fantasy" (ibid., p. 2). Karen's dream embodies this role of fairy tales as "containers for organizing events into meaningful experiences." In many ways the representation of Karen's psyche in her dream reveals her search for the appropriate story, the one which will tell the tale that will both contain and symbolize the issues that she is facing. The fantasy texts in her dream reflect the feeling dimension in narrative; they both embody the confusion she is feeling and point to a way beyond the developmental impasse in which she is caught up.

In this light her blacking out stands for the progressive and selective shedding of levels of identification throughout the dream. Each blacking out leads to a settling into another story, another fairy tale imago or representation of Self. Karen fast-forwards her way through each narrative, reexperiencing the full range of the text, yet focusing finally on the point in it which most concerns her—what happens right after she marries the prince.

Her assumption of the role of Snow White locates the elementary emotions, thoughts, and impulses generated in the initial scene in a context closer to her immediate experience. This narrative involves the family and the issues associated with preadolescence, especially as they concern personal beauty, sexuality, and her mother. Bettelheim, in *The Uses of Enchantment*, emphasizes and amplifies these dimensions to "Snow White." His often programmatic Freudian decoding seems less forced when focused on this dimension of the narrative. He sees Snow White's retreat from and characterization of the conflict with the mother in part as her "projection of one side of an inner conflict onto a parental figure (Bettelheim 1977, p. 211).

In Jungian terms this would be the subjective interpretation of the dream. Her stay in the kingdom of the dwarfs Bettelheim views as an "escape back into a conflict-free latency period, where sex remains dormant and hence adolescent turmoils can be avoided" (ibid.). In his perspective her conflicts with the wicked stepmother all involve the projection of Snow White's own narcissism, her desire to repress her concern with her own personal beauty and budding sexuality. "The story begins," Bettelheim reminds us, "with Snow White's mother pricking her finger so that three drops of blood fall upon the snow. In these images the problems the story sets out to resolve surface: sexual innocence, whiteness, is contrasted with sexual desire, symbolized by the red blood," which could also symbolize menstruation, the physiological signal of this developmental stage (ibid., p. 202). Following this line of reasoning, we can recognize that Snow White's vulnerability to the ploys of the evil queen (the shadow) suggests that "Snow White's conscious intentions are overwhelmed by her desire to have a beautiful coiffure, and her unconscious wish is to be sexually attractive." Bettelheim sees this wish as poisonous to her "in her early, immature adolescent state" (ibid., p. 212).

Bettelheim's emphasis on the dimension of "Snow White" which deals with the wishes and fears of preadolescence, especially the ones which get projected onto the wicked stepmother, focuses on the issues raised in the first part of Karen's dream. The stepmother embodies the personal, collective, and archetypal dimensions of the shadow in a same-sexed figure. In so doing she indicates that the qualities and conflicts embodied in Dracula are now being seen closer to home in a family narrative and in a figure of similar gender. Escape from Dracula has now become escape from the wicked queen. Reinforcing this shadow side of Snow White's sexuality, Bettelheim notes her double nature — white as snow and as red as blood — and argues that it symbolizes the tension between her innocent and erotic aspects. This tension he sees as being resolved when she eats the red (erotic) part of the apple, thus ending her innocence. After that loss, she is placed in the coffin to await the prince and sexual awakening.

Bettelheim's emphasis on the wish-fear dichotomy, however, can easily contaminate this subjective reading of the dream by locating it in the limiting classic paradigm of drive-defense psychology. If we view development as purely a psychosexual matter, then we ignore, as Bettelheim does, Snow White's envious mother who wishes her daughter's death. Such a perspective neglects that Snow White's "regression" could also correspond in Karen's dream to depression, a death of the ego in the face of the mother's destructive envy. It overlooks as well that the dwarfs can be seen as helpful animus figures rather than infantile aspects of the preadolescent ego — helpful ones in Karen's unconscious.

Karen's dream distorts "Snow White" in a manner which has developmental implications. Whereas the dwarfs sat around the coffin and "wept and lamented three whole days" in the original text, they are depicted as dancing and cheering in the dream. Also it is they and not the prince who witness her waking up, and the casket is "like a wooden bed almost," like the bed on which the dreamer is fast asleep. The end is placed at the beginning, and it is the welcoming company of the helpful animus figures of her own psyche that she comes alive to. The dream ego exchanges the original sad scene which foreshadows the role of the prince for one in which she can awake safely from the "sleep" of latency in the company of helpful male figures without the threatening presence of the king's son. He is, though, a less frightening figure than his royal colleague, the Count who carries the shadow of sexual awakening, Dracula. Or an objective reading of Karen's dream at this point might interpret this activity as her searching in her unconscious for the resources (dwarfs, gems and precious stones) with which to handle whatever conflict she is experiencing in her family.

Karen's dream does not directly emphasize the development dimension I have just outlined. But I feel that we can safely infer that the issues raised by the first section in the dream are being reframed for further amplification in Karen's use of subsequent texts. Her associations indicate that her use of "Snow White" in the dream directly involves the wicked stepmother. "She hates Snow White and wants her dead," Karen says, adding that "she hates me because I'm prettier than her." Further, her concern with personal beauty and the implied issue of sexual attractiveness turn up in her associations to the more visual, filmic text of Walt Disney. His movie of Snow White provides her coiffure ("my hair is curled up in the back like in a bun and the front is pulled off the forehead"), and her sister's illustrated book provides the rest of her outfit, the beautiful fancy white ball dress.

"Cinderella" reveals progress in dealing with these conflicts. In this text the daughter is no longer locked in a mortal battle with her stepmother. Instead, "Cinderella" shifts the emphasis onto sibling rivalry, the consequences of which are that she is forced to accept a menial position in the home and to forego a marital future with men of equal or higher status. In both texts a prince rescues the girls and marries them. Cinderella is at a different developmental stage than Snow White. Karen's appearance in her text suggests that she is able to envision the developmental progression Cinderella represents, one closer to mature sexuality.

In "Cinderella," then, the dream ego's relation to the issue of sexuality changes, and the movement from latency into puberty toward mature sexuality seems closer to consciousness, less threatening, and more welcome. Cinderella's conflicts center around her stepmother favoring her two stepsisters. The jealousy of the narcissistic mother is replaced by the ambitious stage mother basking in the reflected glory of her daughter's royal success and replaces the vengeful mother who carries the projection of the Electra daughter's wish to replace her mother in the classical oedipal triangle.

Significantly, Karen takes up the text of "Cinderella" at the point of the transformation, "just when the fairy godmother is changing me into the beautiful ball dress," she says. The emphasis falls not upon the "sleeping," latency in a developmental perspective, the image of being in the coffin. Instead, the dream ego moves closer to the prince and more actively so, however much the fairy godmother provides assistance. The movement in the dream depicts the reluctance of the dream ego in the form of its blacking out, indicating that although there has been some movement beyond latency and toward mature sexuality, she is not yet ready to take the final step. In both narratives Karen's dream ego fast-forwards its way to marriage with the prince. In each it entertains the possibility (marriage to him) and the anxiety (sexual initiation).

Where she locates herself in each text, though, is more important than the fact that she is "moving through it all." In each case she sees herself at a specific point in the plot of each story. What is in focus and not "going extra fast and is blurry" represents the developmental advance as the dream progresses. Like a series of dreams that could easily be widely spaced in time, Karen's condenses the symbolic portrait of her developmental history at this point. The fairy tale texts, like archetypal footnotes in the history of human development, provide navigational charts as well as symbolic representations. The symbolic containers they provide help to locate in a narrative structure what in psychic experience would be the blur produced by anxiety. So Karen, in a sense, redreams the archetypal big dream at the core of the fairy tale narrative, that part of it which transcends the culturally specific content.

Still the time is not yet ripe, and union with the prince must wait. Leaving the third of her texts, Karen finds herself "back with the dwarfs." Returning at this point, it would seem that she needs to do some further digging in the mine of her unconscious. But the prospects seem bright. The helpful dwarfs have not only piled up diamonds, rubies, sapphires, gold, silver, and other gems in "barrels and heaps," but also "many are still on the walls." It would appear that there are quite a few valuable gems and metals in the unconscious. Certainly there seems to be a sufficient amount to "finance" the developmental shift in the offing, even a supply yet to be extracted. Yet the shadow side of this dream image could also indicate that Karen's inner wealth may not be able to support the outer (family) conflict: "the mine collapses on the dwarfs and me."

The final retreat and return may be temporary. In part it is motivated by the battle with the shadow that is still raging above ground. The wicked queen has sent a whole army of "princes" "to go after the dwarfs, because she hates Snow White and wants her dead." The oedipal war is still projected onto the mother; her own sexuality is too threatening yet for Karen to own. But there is progress: now Karen can see the face of the wicked queen, while in the story she said that she could not. The army threatens Karen's infantile preadolescent developmental space, but like the hunts-man who allowed Snow White to escape, they, too, are not com-pletely loyal to the queen they serve.

The psychic drama being played out in this final scene in the dream turns heavily on the attitude of the wicked queen's army. For however much the projection of the shadow is still in place, it has nonetheless migrated from the animus figure of Dracula to be subsequently carried by Karen's own shadow, the wicked step-mother, a *she* whose sexuality has a lethal dimension and whose powerful feelings instigate a war. In fact, the image of war in Karen's dream ranges throughout human history from the knights of the Middle Ages to the American War of Independence to the Civil War of brother against brother. All symbolize Karen's sense of the psychic war raging at this time, and they reveal its different levels. The "knight" side reflects the more settled condi-tion of childhood, a period of settled aristocracy when the rules of conduct were clear and guided the behavior of the knights, "the strong protective type, nice and kind." But as the "war" moves closer to home the issue of independence appears on two levels: between child (America) and parent (England), Snow White's struggle with the wicked stepmother, her war of independence, and between siblings in "Cinderella" (Civil War).

In this final scene the preadolescent world of latency embodied in the fairy tale narratives gets reconstellated in the associations to wars. In both narratives and associations the developmental issues remain the same — independence, auton-omy, mature sexuality. The outcomes of the wars suggested by Karen's associations, along with the "mother load" of gems in the unconscious, are that both victory and reconciliation (or collapse) are in the future. The battle cannot be escaped forever. The mine eventually caves in and an aggressive meeting of conscious and unconscious appears in the future, one that Karen escapes in the time being for the safety of her own bed.

The spell of the wicked queen, in part Karen's projected shadow, controls the knights and soldiers still. As long as she cannot make conscious and integrate her own sexual feelings, she will experience them in projected form and in their shadow aspect as draculean — obsessional, aggressive, enslaving, and destruc-tive. When that spell is broken, however, the animus figures which carry the projection of an aggressive sexuality show great potential for integration. When they no longer embody an uncon-scious attitude which experiences itself as "forced to do it," they can express their true nature as "the 'knight type,' " Karen describes, "the strong protective type, nice and kind, but not *overly* protective." Karen's qualification of the style of the "knight type" leads to the cultural dimension of these fairy tales. For on the objective level all the texts Karen uses, when read on the literal level, lock women into a gender role which puts them in a developmental bind. They are damned if they do progress to mature sexuality, and damned if they do not.

The appearance of Karen in the "Snow White" text can be seen in another way than I viewed it earlier, as awakening in the presence of helpful animus figures. Arrival in that text is arrival in a *casket*. If we see the text in the perspective of a casket, the reluctance to form union with the prince takes on an added dimension. The fear, then, involves the cultural framework in the text which from Karen's perspective sees overprotectiveness as domination by the male. This is a good deal different from the subjective perspective that I have been developing, the one wherein Karen is dominated by her own sexuality which appears in the images of Dracula and the wicked queen. Recall that Karen says she is "in the casket that the dwarfs built for Snow White when they thought she was dead." The image of being thought to be dead characterized Karen's entry into the text of "Snow White" and is present in the way she distorts the narrative.

The casket comes at the end before the prince arrives, not at the beginning when she meets the dwarfs. Insofar as it does come at the beginning, it describes an ambivalence that adds culture in the form of gender role to the anxiety which fuels Karen's reluctance to consummate her marriage to the prince. Karen's transposition of the casket scene avoids the stylized encounter with the prince with all its patriarchal implications. Instead she wakes up on her own in the presence of helpful animus figures, the dwarfs. Perhaps this is because Karen likes not only the conventionally feminine modesty of Snow White and Cinderella ("They weren't proud of their beauty. They were modest"), but also their more "masculine" aggressive behavior when she acknowledges with admiration that "they outsmarted people."

To see resistance in this dream as only an infantile wish to stop time, to deny developmental destiny, confuses the archetypal with the cultural levels in the narratives Karen's unconscious employs. Responding to this ambivalence, feminist critics of these texts, like Jennifer Waelti-Walters, confuse these two levels and see them as mutually exclusive, whereas I see them as complementary. Karen's experience of them in her dream indicates a revisionist perspective at work in her ambivalence toward the role of prince in the cultural dimension of these narratives. Her response shows that the archetypal cores of the narratives are still useful. They image and provide a relation to rather than an identification with the eros seeking expression and integration in a different form and at another level of psychic and biological development.

Identifying this problem, Waelti-Walters comments, in *Fairy Tales and the Female Imagination*, that "it is [her] contention that fairy tales – 'Cinderella,' 'Snow White,' and 'Beauty and the Beast' in particular. . .do not help little girls to achieve autonomy in the way that they help little boys. On the contrary they hold girls back. They offer only security: that of being loved by father or his substitute" (Waelti-Walters 1982, p. 7). Even allowing for the too literalized readings that Waelti-Walters gives these fantasy texts, we must nonetheless take her point and deal with the cultural definitions of gender encoded in them.

Whether or not we see the prince as the animus figure of the masculine contrasexual other she needs to "marry" and thus to integrate, we still are left with the objective, sociocultural dimension of the narrative. That involves passivity, emphasis on beauty as a way to attract men, and becoming the prince's wife. Commenting on this pattern, Waelti-Walters says that "fairy tales teach girls to accept at least a partial loss of identity" (ibid.). Not to see this cultural dimension is to privilege a psychoanalytic discourse to the point of allowing it to obscure the limiting aspects of culture in these texts. In the area of gender, these aspects preserve a dimension of historical time that is no longer relevant to the present. It would seem that Karen, too, senses that partial loss and is understandably "very scared." This may be one way to explain the image of war – a quite uneven one – which her unconscious uses to describe the feeling tone of the struggle with the issue of sexual awakening.

These wars carry the related issues of independence and protection in Karen's description of the men. Describing them and their attitudes, Karen says, "I get the impression that they are under a spell or they wouldn't do this. They are forced to do it." She also notes with reservation their "strong protective type." A tension between independence and protection develops from her observations and, in part, brings Karen's dream to a point of hopeful indeterminancy and irresolution. This indicates a significant tension between these two opposed feelings. Reading this tension as arising because of the potential for conflating the cultural and the archetypal levels in the fairy tale texts, we can find a way out of the feminist position of the double bind.

For Waelti-Walters's reading of these narratives is both too literal and too conservative. Critics like her become entangled in the cultural double bind they criticize. They assume that the text dominates the reader, that it functions as a form of cultural determinism. This view of textual (and therefore cultural) autonomy neglects the work of contemporary reader-response theorists who acknowledge the active role of the reader as well as her idiosyncrasy.[3] To homogenize the reading audience as young girls being offered only security in the form of father love is to deny the dialogic relation between ego and Self as well as the Self's role in individuation.

This is behavioristic thinking in that it diminishes the complex function of archetypes. In this view the concepts of archetype and stimulus are considered synonymous. It is a perspective which privileges the influence of society in the process of conditioning an organism, not an individual: literalism in its most reductive guise. Fairy tale texts, however, are not social and psychological destiny. They are imaginal opportunity. The dialogic relation with them that Karen's unconscious establishes represents a transaction, not an interaction. Narratives like "Snow White" and "Cinderella" have no autonomous meaning, no independent life like a rigid, manipulative personality. If they had, Waelti-Walters would be right. Such texts would be "neurotic" and transactions with them severely limiting. So as Karen's unconscious "reads" these texts in her dream life, her relation to them is not that of a Sleeping Beauty or a Snow White passively awaiting the awakening "kiss" of the text. She does not approve only of the more conventionally "feminine" personality traits of Snow White or Cinderella. In fact she likes and identifies with these young girls in part because of their "masculine," aggressive

---

[3]See, for example, Louise M. Rosenblatt, *The Reader, the Text, the Poem: The Transactional Theory of the Literary Work* (1978); Norman H. Holland, *Poems in Persons: An Introduction to the Psychoanalysis of Literature* (1975); David Bleich, *Subjective Criticism* (1978); Susan R. Suleiman and Inge Crosman, eds., *The Reader in the Text: Essays on Audience and Interpretation* (1980); and Jane P. Tompkins, ed., *Reader-Response Criticism: From Formalism to Poststructuralism* (1980).

characters: "They outsmarted people," Karen commented with admiration. Actively engaged with these texts, Karen's unconscious explores their possibilities.

Her associations indicate that she responds to an archetypal dimension in the characters of both Snow White and Cinderella — the Trickster. In their talent for outsmarting the negative mother figures, both have a measure of control. Tricking creates space between the individual, culture and society. To outsmart others one must know beforehand what they consider smart. So Karen's recognition of this archetypal aspect of Snow White and Cinderella reveals that she sees them as aware of the cultural scripts and codes they are caught up in. She isn't identified exclusively with Snow White or Cinderella, she relates to them through the analogical bond she forms. They are useful to her as metaphors with archetypal resonance. They allow her to explore her experience of Self in an open-ended, not self-limiting fashion. Texts like "Snow White" and "Cinderella" should perhaps be seen less as developmental programs with hidden sexist agendas and more as ones which create a useful tension between the archetypal and cultural dimensions within them. How that tension is resolved is a matter for the dreamer herself to determine.

In this perspective, these fairy tale texts do not force a particular resolution upon those who connect with the archetypal dimensions in them. Resolution comes about in the individual psyche as it moves toward individuation. The process of soul-making lies in the person, not in the text or culture. To argue for the dominance of either is to deny the soul-making power of the Self, to overlook the developmental value of the tensions produced by oppositions both inside and out. It is to reduce the transformative possibility inherent in symbol to recipes for gender roles, to announce a victory for the social ego in an implied argument for behavioral conditioning. To do that denies the autonomy of the Self and the complexity of becoming.

Karen seems aware of this herself when she notes that there are two rides, although she cannot see the second one. Perhaps that is a personality Karen cannot conceive of yet, one that may surface when she can see the second ride. But access to this other possibility requires satisfactory resolution of the conflicts that *Dracula*, "Snow White," and "Cinderella" help her to personify and make conscious.

REFERENCES

Bettelheim, B. 1977. *The Uses of Enchantment.* New York: Vintage Books.

Bleich, D. 1978. *Subjective Criticism.* Baltimore: The Johns Hopkins University Press.

de Castillejo, I. C. 1973. *Knowing Women: A Feminine Psychology.* New York: Putnam's.

Edinger, E. F. 1973. *Ego and Archetype.* Baltimore: Penguin Books.

Goldenberg, N. 1976. A feminist critique of Jung. *Signs* 2,2.

Hillman, J. 1975. *Loose Ends: Primary Papers in Archetypal Psychology.* Dallas: Spring Publications.

Holland, N. H. 1975. *Poems in Persons: An Introduction to the Psychoanalysis of Literature.* New York: W. W. Norton.

Jung, E. 1969. *Anima and Animus.* Dallas: Spring Publications.

Leonard, L. S. 1987. *On the Way to the Wedding: Transforming the Love Relationship.* Boston: Shambhala.

Mattoon, M. A., and Jones, J. 1987. Is the animus obsolete? *Quadrant* 20, 1:5–21.

Rosenblatt, L. M. 1978. *The Reader, the Text, the Poem: The Transactional Theory of the Literary Work.* Carbondale, Ill.: Southern Illinois University Press.

Suleiman, S. R., and Crosman, I., eds. *The Reader in the Text: Essays on Audience and Interpretation.* Princeton, N.J.: Princeton University Press.

Tompking, J. P., ed. 1980. *Reader-Response Criticism: From Formalism to Poststructuralism.* Baltimore: The Johns Hopkins University Press.

von Franz, M-L. 1970. *Interpretation of Fairy Tales.* Dallas: Spring Publications.

Waelti-Walters. 1982. *Fairy Tales and the Female Imagination.* St. Albans, N.Y.: Eden Press.

"Snow White and Rose Red"
Contained Oppositions

Lee Zahner-Roloff

I

We need to peruse and muse over the images of folktale and
myth. . .It is time to retell the familiar stories, to rediscover what
we may already know without fully knowing that we know it – the
many ways in which brotherhood and sisterhood have been lived
and imagined in the past – so that we may reimagine sibling experience for ourselves with as much richness and depth as possible.
(Downing 1988, p. 18)

In the contained and imaginal world which psyche inhabits, perhaps no power to hold psyche in aesthetic arrest is greater than
the fairy tale. In the unerring simplicity of image and event, the
movement of the fairy tale draws the hearer or reader into the
deepest satisfaction of knowing "the rightness," "the trueness,"
"the congruence" of the tale told and the knowledge gained.

It is the fairy tale's deceptive "surface" that is the source of
all delight and, so it would seem, so utterly unpretentious that
protracted interpretations are something of an affront. The visual analogue to the fairy tale is best exemplified by two-
dimensional icons and Byzantine paintings. In these visual experiences, the surface of the painting is flat, lacking perspective.
Fairy tales are very much like these paintings. All but absent, the
psychological narrator presents the simplest and most direct
images in two-dimensional language devoid of psychological dis-

course. Very little of that below the surface is given. The depth of the tale is in the perceiver's projections and identifications with the elements. Much like contemporary television and motion-picture cartoons, the child's delight is all in the surface. It is the adult's perception that worries the images into values, themes, cultural implications. As entertainments, fairy tales survive precisely because of the surface's facility to create realms of imaginal projection for each generation of hearers, and now, in the twentieth century, viewers as well. However, all that is nascent in the child's ability to develop consciousness is presented by the unassailable rightness of the fairy-tale imagination.

Children know these elements of a fairy tale without the abstract vocabulary used to identify what it is that makes a fairy tale so effective. Knowledge is in the rightness of image, in the movement of episodes, in the correctness of the tale's eventual conclusion. This is the elementary psychology of all fairy tales. What is so striking about "Snow White and Rose Red" is that its utter simplicity so guilelessly understood by a child often can elude an adult reader into either dismissing or overpsychologizing the tale. "Snow White and Rose Red" is a tale about a mother and her daughters—in short, the feminine. The tale suggests an awakening of feminine consciousness from simple trust to feminine wit, of finding the fullness of a feminine potential. Finally, the "tale telling" is a discovery by the feminine of what she needs to learn about the masculine, at the same time retaining an appropriate playfulness to *all* that is masculine. It is a tale of contained oppositions. As preserved by the Brothers Grimm, the tale first recounts how a widow and her two daughters, Snow White and Rose Red, living alone in an isolated cottage, pass their days.

Snow White and Rose Red

S now White and Rose Red lived in a world free of fear, moving about in this world with delight and wonderment. One evening, unexpectedly, a bear arrives at the door of the cottage, and because it is winter, the bear is invited into the household. It remains for all of the winter months, playing with the children. On the first note of spring, the bear announces that it has to leave, much to the sadness of the daughters. As it leaves, the bear's fur catches on the bolt to the door, revealing to Snow White a glint of gold shining beneath the fur.

The daughters are returned to their world of tasks by performing those determined by their mother. While attempting to perform these simple errands, Snow White and Rose Red encounter a grotesque and thoroughly disagreeable dwarf, who, on three separate occasions, calls upon the daughters to rescue him from difficulties into which he has fallen: his beard catches in a crevice of a tree, it becomes tangled in a fishing line, and, in the third mishap, he is seen being carried aloft by an eagle. The dwarf, never grateful for being rescued, carps and cavils about the carelessness that Snow White and Rose Red seem to inflict upon him.

After the third rescue, the girls note that he has a sack full of precious stones that he takes with him as he slips away into his hole. While returning home to their mother from the third task she had sent them upon, they "catch" the dwarf examining his precious stones as the evening sun shines upon them. The dwarf, enraged by their staring and having been exposed, curses them. At this moment the bear reappears. The dwarf is so terrified that he pleads for his life by begging the bear "to eat the two wicked girls." The bear takes no heed. With his paw, and with a single blow, he kills the dwarf. In the moment of killing, the hide falls from the bear revealing a king's son clothed in gold. The king's son had been bewitched by the wicked dwarf who had stolen his treasures. In a rapid denouement, Snow White marries the king's son, Rose Red marries his brother, and the faithful mother lives peacefully with her children for many years.

In its tersest summation, this is the action of the tale.

The tale has three movements of delight and instruction: the first of Eden-lived/Eden-found; the second of knowledge lived/knowledge found; the third in the uses of wit and the finding of love. In these three movements, Snow White and Rose Red leave Eden and its limits of innocence, enter into the world with wit and intelligence, and find the completion of a feminine journey in a psychological and physical relationship with the discovered and released masculine. Obviously, the tension between a literalism of the lived feminine and a symbolic interpretation of the feminine journey from innocence to knowledge is one that each reader must reconcile.

The provocative beginning of the tale is one that a casual reader might not fully entertain as significant; yet it is so pertinent to all the follows that it deserves special noting. The tale begins, "There was once a poor widow who lived in a lonely cottage" (*The Complete Grimm's Fairy Tales*, p. 664). The key word is *widow*, one who lacks a husband, and, by extension to Snow White and Rose Red, those who lack a father. Living in a lonely cottage is living in isolation, away, distant from community. It is this isolation that begins the story: the self-containedness of mother and daughters *without the presence of the masculine in husband or father*. By implication and indirectness, it is the wisdom of the feminine that guides, directs, permits, leads, educates from this situation. And who is it that is guided, directed, and given the permissions to explore the world? The contained oppositions of the two daughters: one is self-contained, contented to remain at home, possessed by a love of reading, and by nature quiet and gentle (Snow White); the other is curious, related to nature in all its facets, exploring the world, and by character ready to act, to probe, to investigate (Rose Red). These descriptions are the most elementary and facile definitions of introversion and extraversion found in folk literature. They are propensities of all human behavior here represented as viable, true, natural personalities. And, they are color coded in such a way as to be unerring: white and red. Further, each is mutually dependent upon the other, pledged to support, honor, and protect the other, as when Snow White states to her sister, "We will not leave each other." To which Rose Red responds, "Never so long as we live" (ibid.). These statements are as striking, as simple and as satisfying of containment as can be found in the wisdom of folk literature.

How Snow White and Rose Red live in their contained isolation is even more compelling. The widowed mother has created in her daughters a complete and total trust of the world of nature. Nothing is prohibited in this Edenic place. The girls are free to wander in the forest, their innocence is shared with all instinctual life, "no beasts did them any harm, but came close to them trustfully" (ibid.). Learning and listening to the songs of the birds, trusting night and its mysteries, these innocents are given permission by the mother to be in natural concert with day and night, flower and animal.

Here, the two aspects of the virginal are given imaginal assurance: the virginal nature of instinctual life, its nature and its epiphanies; and the human virginity of inexperience with others, and the awakening to human sexuality denoting a profound change in consciousness. There is no danger in the world for this virginal bliss because there is the presence of a guardian angel that protects from "falling off into an abyss," the protective masculine who prevents "falling from a cliff." This guardian spirit is the unconscious masculine within the virginal consciousness, not conscious, but protective. The mother knows of this for when the girls tell her of the experience of "sleeping near the edge of a cliff," the mother informs them that "it must have been the guardian angel" who protected them (p. 665). The mother knows and it is she who elicits trust.

The authority of this tale is precisely the maternal grounding of trust, in the maternal instruction of earth's treasures, in the wisdom of giving identity to opposite dispositions. The first part of the tale is the fullest expression of all that is virginal, the intactness of nature, the unsundered, the uncut, the effortless play of all nature in harmony. The setting provides the background to the two daughters whose virginity is the most poignant in all fairy-tale literature.

The exploration of Eden-lived/Eden-found concludes with endings and new beginnings, the ending of summer and the sudden beginning of winter, for such is the necessity of collapsing time in fairy tales. Summer's Edenic time is over, the fire is laid, the kettles are polished to shine like gold, the mother reads to the girls on a winter's night as "close by them lay a lamb upon the floor, and behind them upon a perch sat a white dove with its head hidden beneath its wings" (ibid.). The intactness of the feminine is complete, the security of the guiding and permissive mother omnipresent, as the lamb and the dove slumber. It is Snow White who is asked to bolt the door against the winter night. This is the most natural function of the introverted spirit – to know the safety of all that is within. Safety and security are not conditions that always welcome change. It is at this moment in the story, however, that change is about to be announced; it is time for growth, for a new knowledge to be found and lived. To live with innocence alone is unacceptable, for in innocence there is no shadow. In an awakening, there is a transformation; in transformation, there is new life. A new life is the promise of the initiation from innocence to adulthood, precisely the journey undertaken by Snow White and Rose Red.

It is the ear that captures the indelible accuracy of image in fairy tales. In reading fairy tales, the eye can be too quick, too facile, too scanning to register the simple directness of what image is accomplishing through the telling of the tale. In the first part, for example, the girls are precisely named and given oppositional personalities. The mother is by her actions a loving mother, and not an abstraction of a "loving mother." Even small imaginal details are presented to capture *the directional change of the tale's telling*. When, for example, winter has come and the enclosure of life has taken place, the prefiguring of the masculine is introduced subtly by the lighting of the *fire*, the polishing of the kettle which shines like *gold*, and the direct commands to "bolt the door," the bolt being the instrument which will act to reveal the masculine *gold* imprisoned and enchanted in a bear's form.

This native intelligence to telescope the psychology of fairy tales is present in every fairy tale, and nowhere more effortlessly presented than in "Snow White and Rose Red." Time-factored imagery (morning, noon, night; spring, summer, fall, and winter, etc.) announces to the listener what is needed to be known in both the literal movement of the tale as well as in its metaphoric and symbolic reaches. Thus it is that the second part begins with winter, but specifically a *winter's night*. Further, all that has been missing by the absence of the masculine is revealed by a single pronoun. The tale begins the second part with this sentence, "One evening, as they were thus sitting comfortably together, someone knocked at the door as if he wished to be let in" (p. 665). What is there in a knock that makes it particularly masculine, one may ask? The logic of a fairy tale is impeccably simple: *because it is necessary*. Why, one may ask, is it "necessary"? The masculine that had been absent has arrived suddenly to fill that absence. Of all words in fairy tales, none is more important than *suddenly*, for life is shaped and directed as much by the sudden as by that which is planned. It is the immediate and unexpected which shape and redirect our lives from our intended plans. It is suddenness that delivers us into consciousness. What we learn in certain fairy tales is that certain sudden events are necessary for growth, change, and maturation. In the lives of the two girls, it is the propitious moment for the arrival of the instinctual masculine.

Just as Snow White had been asked to *bar* the door, the mother asks Rose Red to *unlock* it. As she unlocks it, Rose Red thinks to herself that it is probably a poor man, but it is not. It is a bear that stretches his broad black head within the door.

The psychological reaction to this moment is precise: Rose Red screams, Snow White hides. The bear simply says, "Do not be afraid, I will do you no harm! I am half frozen, and only want to warm myself a little beside you" (p. 665). The mother admonishes her daughters to come out of hiding, to end their fears, and to welcome this new energy into the home.

What is present is the wisdom of a mothering instinct that is not afraid, that allays the fears of the innocent daughters, that welcomes the changes this new energy will bring into the lives of Snow White and Rose Red. In the psychology of the fairy tale, what is learned is that when the instinctual arrives, *it means no harm.* Clearly all that was Edenic in its unconsciousness in the first part is now changed in the second: the introduction of the specifically instinctual, positive aspect of the masculine in its yet unrevealed totality. There are to be new knowledges learned and lived.

What the feminine learns in its introduction to the instinctual masculine is remarkably simple: *be playful.* "They tugged his hair with their hands, put their feet upon his back and rolled him about, or they took a hazel-switch and beat him, and when he growled they laughed" (p. 666). In the healthiest of initial lessons, the first is to be playful, joyous, exploratory in the new awakening. And to bring no harm. "Leave me alive, children, Snow-White, Rose-Red, will you beat your wooer dead?" (ibid.). Note that at this exploratory edge, the girls are addressed as "children." The transit to womanhood is just beginning.

At the conclusion of this winter's play, the winter of childhood's last innocence, spring arrives. What the tale makes explicit is that it is the introverted principle that has made its connection to the masculine and its instinctual promise. As the bear prepares to leave, he addresses Snow White, "Now I must go away, and cannot come back for the whole summer." "Where are you going, then, dear bear?" asks Snow White (p. 666). The bear's reply is that it must go to guard its treasure from wicked dwarfs who, while kept underground by the winter's cold, are free to pry and steal the treasures of the masculine during the summer. As the bear leaves, one of the most magical moments of knowledge learned and lived is shared through the experience of Snow White. She is sorry at the bear's departure, and it is she who unbolts the door, she who but a few months ago had hidden at the apparition of the bear's presence at the door. As the bear leaves, his fur catches on the bolt, and a small piece is torn off, "and it seemed to Snow-White as if she had seen gold shining through it, but she was not sure about it" (p. 668). This hint, this glint, this catching of "something" outside herself she cannot be sure she saw.

The second part ends on this perception. Nothing can be the same because something exists, possibly, "beyond the lonely cottage." Once again, it will be the mother who will lead her daughters into the world through what appear to be innocuous tasks. It is through these tasks that the innate wit of the feminine is revealed, and the instrument of these revelations is the negative masculine energy of the "dwarfed man."

The third part in the initiatory process of Snow White and Rose Red presents a surprising turn of events. In this section of the tale, the girls suddenly encounter the inversion of masculine energy and potential. Why the diversion with the dwarf? Why the three episodes of apparent triviality (the trivia of inner knowledge learned and lived)? While the unassailability of the fairy tale cannot be doubted, the rational mind must not excuse easily what would appear unnecessary, uselessly diversionary. What is enchanted and locked in the body of a bear (a natural masculine instinctuality) is in distinction to a dwarfed and misshapen form (a fussy, negative, hoarding, retentive masculine attitude). The cool logic of the two young women who encounter this distorted behavior of the irascible and unattractive dwarf is a necessary lesson for all awakening women. It is the discovery of perception, intellect, and rationality: the inner masculine.

The inner masculine capabilities are a complementary addition to the warmth and understanding of the nurturing feminine, the feeling side of the feminine. The feminine that perceives, evaluates, and acts has the power to cope with the dwarfed masculine expressed as arbitrary, illogical, ungrateful, thankless. It is this form of the masculine that steals and robs from the natural instinctual aspects of the masculine consciousness (the dwarf versus the bear/prince). This is as much a literal reality as an inner one, a phenomenon as necessary for men to learn as for women. How does this negative aspect appear in the story, and how does it function?

Snow White and Rose Red have three tasks to perform for the dwarf and a fourth encounter with him. Each of the three tasks poses a problem and each is solved, but never to the satisfaction of the dwarf. The fourth encounter is the confrontation with the redemptive masculine force of the bear/prince. How are these revealed in the story? In each instance, the mother ostensibly sends her daughters on a quest: to get fire wood, to obtain a dish of fish, and, finally, to purchase needles, thread, laces, and ribbons.

On the first quest, the girls find the dwarf with his beard caught in the crevice of a tree. It is Rose Red who inquires what is wrong; it is Snow White who provides the solution to the problem. Once again, the contained oppositions of the two girls function in concert, Rose Red representing a relationship to the outer world and Snow White offering the solution from her position of observation. (This will be true for the first and second encounter, and implicit in the third.) The solution to the dwarf's problem is to cut the beard and release the wretched little man. In this he is not grateful, for the release has been at the cost of shortening his white beard.

In the second encounter, his beard is tangled in a fishing line at the end of which is a large fish threatening to pull the dwarf into the water. Once again, Snow White's solution is to cut the beard, freeing the dwarf and, at the same time, unleashing his scorn and ridicule at the radical nature of the solution.

In the third encounter, the dwarf, about to be carried off into the air by an eagle, is rescued by the two girls who hang on to his legs. Released from the clutches of the bird, the dwarf falls to the earth, bruising himself. Again, his carping criticism is, "Could you not have done it more carefully?" (p. 670). It is the intelligence of the girls which rescues the dwarf in each case, while the dwarf, or the arrested masculine reaction, never thanks, acknowledges, rewards, or honors. The tale is revealing in what the feminine learns from this attitude, wretched as it is. "The girls, who by this time were used to his ingratitude, went on their way and did their business in the town" (ibid.). In contrast to the bear/prince, with the dwarf there is no play, few playful moments, little tolerance, and no understanding. This is as crippled and grotesque a masculine attitude as anyone might have.

These three encounters have a remarkable subscript. Recall that in the first part the fire was laid just prior to the arrival of the bear/prince; in the second part, the encounters with the dwarf include earth (the beard caught in the tree), water (the line caught by the fish), and air (the dwarf caught by the eagle). In the subscript, the feminine learns something from each of the four elements, fire, earth, water, and air. In the structure of the story, it is fire that leads to the glint of the gold, and it is earth, water, and air from which the masculine is rescued. Being caught, pulled, or carried away by any negative force requires quick action and resourcefulness. Snow White and Rose Red reveal the innate ability to exercise judgment which keeps them grounded, wiser, and quite self-contained.

In the last encounter, Snow White and Rose Red witness the battle and conflict between contrasting masculine attitudes. Coming upon the dwarf unexpectedly, they catch him prizing and observing his hoard of precious jewels, stolen from the prince. In this encounter, two contrasting masculine forces "fight it out" and the enchanted bear/prince does kill that power which would be so destructive and selfish. Redeemed from his spell, the king's son chooses Snow White as his bride; Rose Red is married to his brother. The echo of promises is heard: "We will not leave each other." "Never so long as we live." Succinctly, what these young women learn is that, first, the masculine cannot remain an "enchanted instinctuality," but neither should it be a distorted, ungrateful, argumentative attitude. Both extremes are unacceptable. In an astonishing economy of inverted masculine energies, the lesson of the tale is that both can be transformed. As a matter of image, it is the dwarfed masculine attitude that enchants and imprisons the instinctual. A woman's relationship to the masculine is in both body and soul. The true treasure of the masculine, that which is most precious, cannot be hoarded with an improper attitude, a crippling amassing of fortune for its own ends. When the dwarf unwittingly empties his precious hoard for the girls to see, the bear "suddenly" appears. The spirit of inversion is ended, the imprisoned instinctuality is released in its human form.

There are some significant images mentioned in the earliest passages of the story that demand discussion. The mother has two rose bushes planted by the door of that "lonely cottage" which was the Edenic beginning of this initiatory journey. The white and red rose bushes from which flowers were picked are emblematic representations of the daughters, and these return at the conclusion of the story. "The old mother lived peacefully and happily with her children for many years. She took the two rose-trees with her, and they stood before her window, and every year bore the most beautiful roses, white and red" (p. 671). This ending is not about the daughters "who lived happily ever after," but about the widowed mother who has given her daughters the natural grace to be in the world, the capacity to explore and welcome the instinctual, and the wisdom to be independent as persons. What she retains and keeps is not her daughters but emblematic representations of them. She has given her daughters to the world and she has kept for herself their living emblematic presence. The daughters have not become vegetative beings, lost to the world in an inappropriate innocence and possession by the mother. Rather, they have moved from Eden, they have welcomed knowledge, they have expressed their own intelligences, and they have found and married the masculine. This is the idealization of fulfillment, of freedom, of being in the world.

II

Even in my second analysis, my mother appeared only as a somewhat oversolicitous woman with good intentions who had tried to do her best. It didn't fit in with the training or ethical attitudes of either of my therapists for them to acknowledge that her pedagogic efforts had served *her* interests and the conventional ideas of her day while ruthlessly violating her child, whom she considered as her property. Thus, in my second analysis, I still took pains to try to be understanding of my mother, to forgive her for her subtle psychological cruelty, which kept appearing in my dreams, and to ascribe its origins to my own failings. These "failings" consisted above all of the questions I asked and of my natural childhood needs for protection, closeness, understanding, and responsiveness. Since she was a brilliant pedagogue, she succeeded perfectly in crushing my true feelings and needs in such an imperceptible way that neither I nor anyone else realized what had happened. By an early age I had become a considerate, protective, understanding daughter who always gave priority to her mother's well-being and safety. It wasn't until many years later that I became aware I had a right to needs of my own. (Miller 1986, p. 5)

A fairy tale holds the images of creation in psyche. Unassailable in their rightness, in opposition to the human lived experience of daily events, they hold another way, another vision, another possibility. We live with memories of human mothers. The courage by which Alice Miller writes of the specificity of her relationship to her mother is a recognition that her life has not been a fairy tale. Anyone, male or female, would welcome a mother like the maternal force in "Snow White and Rose Red." Or, for that matter, a father who would demonstrate the idealization of permitting children to take a journey into life in the act of purity that the fairy tale represents. Would, in a mantic moment of asking, Alice Miller have been able to write of her own mother in such a way if she had experienced the creative mothering in "Snow White and Rose Red"? It is what she would have desired, it is by implication what she is imagining in her own corrective acts of consciousness. Life is not an arc of purest release. It is a daily struggle with all that is dwarfed and distorted, hoarding and prizing for its own possessiveness the diamonds and jewels thieved and purloined. What Snow White and Rose Red encounter with the dwarfed and distorted is every person's daily confrontation, consciously and unconsciously. Whether it is a man embodying the dwarfed and stunted reactions to life, or a woman developing a personality dominated by those masculine attitudes and behaviors which hinder relationship to a more natural and instinctual masculine energy, the tale addresses each. A childhood is an incremental loss of innocence; adulthood cannot be imagined as a longing for an illusion. Innocence is virginity, an unconscious state of containment unsullied by acts of consciousness. If the fairy tale leads its perceiver anywhere, it leads to the resurrection of playfulness, of an attitude that will not "kill a wooer dead." A dwarfed attitude enthralls, captures, and threatens playfulness, it robs life of jewels and settles for hoarding and hiding. And, most profoundly, wise parenting knows this. Second only to incest, the worst is to hide a child from the world, to create fear and apprehension for any change, to deny the instinctual fulfillment of the person. "Snow White and Rose Red" is a miracle of the Germanic imagination, and perhaps it is one of the more interesting representations of the teller "herself," that wise old woman who performed for the Brothers Grimm.

REFERENCES

Downing, C. 1988. *Psyche's Sisters: Re-Imagining the Meaning of Sisterhood.* New York: Harper-Row.
Miller, A. 1986. *Pictures of a Childhood.* H. Hannum, trans. New York: Farrar, Straus and Giroux.
The Complete Grimm's Fairy Tales. New York: Pantheon Books, 1944.

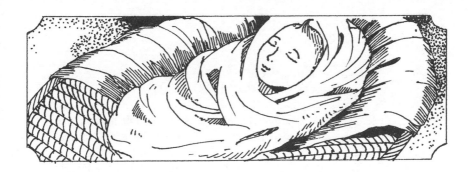

"*Śunaḥśepa*" and "*Akanandun*"
Eating the Son and the Indian Father's Mid-Life Initiation

Alfred Collins

Fathers and sons in the world of patrilineal imagination might be said both to share and to dispute a common self, one which is passed down the generations like an English family seat entailed to the rightful heir of its last inhabitant. Like the house, a man's self from this perspective is only partly his own; like the house, it will fall into ruin unless a son succeeds to its benefits and obligations. The psychic and interpersonal turmoil for fathers and sons in such a world – still, in part, our own – can be intense. The son may feel compelled to live a self not his own as his life drains into the decrepit veins of an old father. The father sees himself slowly losing what is most his own, as the son takes over his place and his vitality. Each may revolt against the mythologem of the patrilineal self, the son by rejecting the father and his self, the father by attempting to claim that self as his sole property or freehold and to treat the son as only an organ of himself, to be disposed of as needed to preserve and enhance himself. Successful resolutions of these conflicts are difficult, but are reached in some Western myths and fairy tales. The two Indian tales which follow fall within this complex and offer a somewhat new way of viewing it.

Śunaḥśepa (Dog's Tail)
(Vedic India, 1000 B.C.)

H ariścandra was a king who had no son, though he had one hundred wives. Once the king addressed the sage Narada, who lived in his house: "All creatures, both beasts and men, wish for a son. Tell me, Narada, what fruit is gained through having a son?"

Narada answered the king with ancient religious verses (gāṭha-s) that tell the son's value to his father: "A father pays his debt to the gods through his son, and gains immortality through him. A man enters his wife as semen and in the tenth month is reborn from her as the son. Thus in the son the father's self (ātman) is born from the self, and like a well-provisioned boat he carries the father to the far shore of death. This is the broad, well-trodden road where those who have sons walk free from sorrow."

Narada then told the king to beg the god Varuṇa for a son, promising in return to sacrifice the boy to the god as soon as he was born. Hariścandra did this, and a son, Rohita, was born. But instead of sacrificing him, the king said to Varuṇa, "An animal is fit for sacrifice when it is ten days old. Let him reach that age before I sacrifice him to you." Varuṇa agreed.

When Rohita was ten days old, Hariścandra said to Varuṇa, "An animal is fit for sacrifice when its teeth come. Let his teeth come first and then I will sacrifice him." Again Varuṇa agreed. Hariścandra stalled the god several more times, and when the boy was a teenager, he tried one last ploy: "A man of the warrior class is fit for sacrifice only after receiving his weapons. Let me wait until then to sacrifice him."

When Rohita had been invested with his arms, Hariścandra sorrowfully resigned himself to the sacrifice. He said to his son, "My dear, I will sacrifice you to the one who gave you to me." Rohita said "No," took his bow, and fled to the forest where he wandered for a year.

Varuṇa was angry and bound Hariścandra with his noose, making his belly swell with dropsy. When Rohita heard of this, he left the forest and entered a village, where he met the god Indra in human disguise. Indra told him, "There is no happiness for a man who does not roam, Rohita; in society a man becomes a sinner, so wander!"

Persuaded by Indra, Rohita did not return home but wandered in the forest for a second year. Again he entered a village and met

Indra, who once more urged him to continue wandering. In this way five years passed; each year Rohita entered a village and was instructed by Indra in the virtues of wandering in the forest. During the sixth year he met Ajīgarta, who was starving, in the forest. Rohita offered Ajīgarta one hundred cows in exchange for one of his three sons to serve as his substitute in the sacrifice to Varuṇa. Ajīgarta sold his middle son, Śunaḥśepa (Dog's Tail). Rohita returned home with the boy.

At the sacrifice, they could find no one willing to bind the boy to the sacrificial stake. His father, Ajīgarta, however, agreed to do it for another hundred cows. Then no one would perform the ritual killing. Again Ajīgarta volunteered to do it for one hundred more cows. Like Rohita, however, Śunaḥśepa refused the role of sacrificial victim and approached the gods to save himself. He honored one god after another and was set free from the post; at the same time, King Hariścandra's bonds fell away and his belly shrank back to normal size.

Śunaḥśepa then sat beside the sage Viśvamitra and refused to return to his father Ajīgarta, despite the pleas of both his parents. Śunaḥśepa said, "Not even among Śudras [the lowest class of society] has anything like this been seen, that you raised a knife against your son. You preferred three hundred cows to me!" Ajīgarta repented his deed, but Śunaḥśepa stood firm and accepted Viśvamitra's offer to make him the "first born" among his own hundred sons. IIe was given the new name Devārata (God Given) by the sage.

Viśvamitra's older sons, on hearing of this, were angry that their father would install a stranger above them. Viśvamitra cursed these sons to have the lowest, outcaste orders of men as their descendants. His younger sons, who accepted Devārata, were blessed by Viśvamitra: "You will be rich in cattle and children, because you have made me rich in offspring by consenting to my wish."

Akanandun the Only Son
(folktale collected in contemporary India)

There once lived a poor Brahman and his wife. They had seven daughters but no sons, and in spite of much prayer and good works, no son came. The poor Brahman soon began to reason that his bad luck was the result of many sins committed in a previous life.

One day a holy beggar (*sannyasi*) came to the Brahman's house seeking alms. The Brahman invited him in and showed him great hospitality. The visitor was pleased and soon asked if he could do anything in return. The Brahman and his wife related their story. Hearing their sadness at having no son, the beggar was moved with pity, and said to the Brahman, "Do not grieve! You will have a son, but it will be on one condition." The Brahman was overwhelmed with emotion and interrupted, saying, "I will agree to any condition whatsoever. Only let me have a son!"

The *sannyasi* then looked sternly into the eyes of the Brahman and into those of his wife and said, "You will have to return the boy when he is twelve years old." Then without waiting for the Brahman's answer, he suddenly disappeared. Nine months later a son was born. This event so overjoyed the couple that they almost forgot the harsh condition the beggar had set.

The young Brahman was soon given the name Akanandun, meaning "only son." He quickly grew to be a beautiful and very intelligent young boy. His mother and father showered much love and affection on him. And his sisters loved him even more. They would not let him out of their sight, even for a short while. When Akanandun reached the age of five, he was sent to school. There he proved to be very clever in his studies, and he was admired by friends and teachers alike. At the age of ten the family celebrated .iis sacred thread ceremony with great pomp. This ritual entitled him to a second, or spiritual, birth. But finally the day arrived when Akanandun was twelve years old.

One fine morning, when Akanandun was getting ready for school, the saintly beggar suddenly appeared at the door once again and asked, "Where is Akanandun? Return him to me. Have you forgotten your promise?" The Brahman answered, "Oh holy man! I stand by my word," but he was in tears. Nonetheless he soon brought Akanandun before the guest. The saint then said, "Give the boy a ritual bath and wrap him in new clothes." The couple gave Akanandun a bath. It was a bath of tears. They also dressed him in new clothes and brought him to the stranger.

The saintly beggar then asked for a knife. When this was provided, the beggar swiftly cut off Akanandun's head. Then slowly and carefully, like an expert butcher, he also cut off the limbs and other body parts. Seeing her only son torn to bits in this way, the mother soon fainted. The sisters wept and beat their breasts. They tore out their hair. Indeed the whole village came to know of something which they had never heard of or seen in their lives before.

Soon after cutting Akanandun into many pieces, the beggar asked the couple to wash and purify the kitchen. He then asked them to cook the little bits that had been Akanandun's body. Amidst sounds of wailing so intense that they could have melted stones, the butchered Akanandun was boiled.

Next the half-dead mother was asked by the beggar to taste this preparation, to see if it had enough salt. She did this. And as if that was not enough, the beggar then ordered that the cooked meat be served to both parents and also the sisters and to any other kinsmen who were present. But he also asked that one share of the preparation be set aside in the name of Akanandun. Once this had been done, the beggar gave the order for everyone to begin eating. In horror, everyone present heard the sound of a roar in their hearts and in the sky. It was as if the earth and the oceans had opened up. They felt day turn into night. The animals and birds stopped breathing. Every star which once shone in the sky disappeared.

Suddenly the *sannyasi* asked the couple to call Akanandun's name and to ask him to come and take his food. This made things even worse. No one could understand the purpose of such a joke. So they ignored the request. But the beggar, true to his plan, was serious. He repeated his order: "Call Akanandun. Call him and ask him to take his food. Do what I say." One of the sisters, fearing the wrath of the beggar, finally obeyed. After mustering all her strength, she cried out in a small voice, "Akanandana, Akanandana," and lo! Akanandun suddenly appeared before his family, dressed neatly, smiling, and holding his bag of books. No one present could believe their eyes. The mother, the father, and all the sisters broke into smiles. They began to kiss and to hug Akanandun. Suddenly the *sannyasi* disappeared, along with all the cooked food. The birds started to fly again and animals began to move and to breathe. Daylight reappeared on the horizon and everything returned to normal. After this, Akanandun lived a long life with his parents.

In Western depth psychology, the theme of male initiation has usually been located within one or more of three scenarios: separation of the adolescent son from the mother (or Mother); fighting and defeating an evil father figure; and ritual impregnation with the virile essence of the good father (or Fathers), which unites a boy with his masculine heritage. The absence of these "rites" or their failure leads to the tragedy of the "uninitiated male," who wanders unattached to his patrilineage but secretly bound to Mother, a familiar pattern in the narcissistic personality of our time.

The Indian tradition offers a somewhat different perspective on patrilineal initiation, while also incorporating similar themes. If we stretch a net between these two Indian tales, separated in time by 3,000 years, and cast it wide enough to include two other stories which we will consider briefly later, we will find that they suggest a role for the son as agent in the mid-life *father's* initiation, as well as being the recipient of the male parent's fatherly self-substance. They also suggest the extreme ambivalence that Indian fathers, at least, have for their sons, at once depending on them for the prolongation of their sense of self beyond death and fearing a *loss* of self as the older man's vital energies decline and, as it were, flow into the son.

"Akanandun," a folktale, is evidently a simpler story than "Śunaḥśepa," which has been elaborated by its Brahmanical authors; nevertheless, there are several parallels between the stories that suggest they are addressing the same underlying themes. Most striking is, of course, the sacrifice of an only son required as the condition for receiving the son in the first place. Both Hariścandra and the poor Brahman are sonless, and both approach the gods to remedy this inauspicious condition. Each is granted his wish, but is required to return his son to the one who gave him, a holy beggar (*sannyasi*) in the case of the Brahman, Varuṇa (the king of the gods) in Hariścandra's story.

An apparent difference is that Akanandun is to be returned to the *sannyasi* at age twelve, while Hariścandra is supposed to surrender Rohita at birth. Through his cleverness at casuistical argument, however, Hariścandra convinces Varuṇa to wait until the boy receives the arms of the warrior class. This occurs at adolescence, so in fact each son is to be returned at this same stage of life. Another nondifference is the religious-ritual atmosphere of the Śunaḥśepa story, which occurs in the midst of the ritual literature of ancient India, the Brāhmaṇas. While Akanandun is not sacrificed at one of the Great Vedic rites (which are no longer practiced in modern India), several things make it clear that his death at the *sannyasi's* hands is a religious sacrifice of the later, Hindu type: 1) Akanandun is given a ritual bath and is dressed in new clothes; 2) the kitchen is purified before the pieces of his body are cooked; and 3) the cooked meat of Akanandun's body is fed to his family like *prasāda*, the ritually blessed food that is shared among the worshippers at a Hindu temple rite after being first offered to the god.

The biggest difference between the two stories is that Rohita refuses to be sacrificed, as does his replacement Śunaḥśepa. A father–son conflict, not expressed in Akanandun's tale, is suggested by this refusal. The traditional verses recited by Narada on the subject of fathers and sons point to the nature of this conflict. In the traditional Vedic way of understanding the father–son relationship, which is still dominant in contemporary India, the son is a continuation of the father's self (ātman). His life prolongs the father into the future, and even after the father's death, he continues to support him in heaven via the ancestral offering (śrāddha).

The problem implicit in this lies in the understanding of "selfhood," for it is not easy to see how the son can prolong the father's self while also developing as a self in his own right. The "physiological" theory of rebirth expressed by Narada in "Śunaḥśepa" emphasizes father–son continuity and leads to the possible negative consequence of the father overcontrolling the son's life and also becoming overly dependent on him. The result can be to stunt the son's development and to limit his selfhood to being no more than an extension of the father's.

On the other hand, limits to the father's control of the son are recognized, and Ajīgarta clearly oversteps them when he sells his son for food and then offers to bind and slay him for more food. It is as if the starving father were literally to eat his son in order to preserve his own life; the absurdity of this is recognized in our story which works to find a resolution that will allow the son some value in his own right while still performing his traditional role of prolonging the father and saving him from annihilation.

Initially, this resolution requires the son to act in a way that denies his father's wishes, as do Rohita and Śunaḥśepa when they run away from sacrifices that would benefit their father. They are thus to some degree "bad" sons and parallel their fathers who act badly toward them.

"Śunaḥśepa" thus operates by opposing "good" and "bad" fathers and sons, and tries to find a way to reconcile them. In this it is partially successful, and the dramatic action moves toward initiation and individuation in the original father–son pair, Hariścandra and Rohita, and especially in the other son, Śunaḥśepa. Schematically:

	Initiated	Undergoing Initiation	Uninitiated
Fathers	Viśvamitra	Hariścandra	Ajīgarta
Sons	Viśvamitra's younger sons	Rohita, Śunaḥśepa	Viśamitra's older sons

Bad, uninitiated fathers attempt to use up ("eat") the son's physical and psychic self-substance to prolong their own ego life, while bad sons refuse to defer to the father's legitimate need for spiritual renewal. Conversely, good fathers in Vedic India recognize the duty to transmit their mortal substance to their sons at death, and good sons return this as spiritual substance which supports the father's nonphysical existence in the afterlife.

Bad fathers and overly deferential sons are a common theme in Indian culture and society; this has been called the "Laius complex" by A. K. Ramanujan (1983), after Oedipus's father. A reversal of the Oedipus complex, however, does not completely capture the flavor of the bad-father theme, which is at least as much *pre*-oedipal and narcissistic, dealing with the effects of nurturance and its absence on the sense of self. Similarly, good father–son relations involve feeding and its analogs.

For instance, at the *śrāddha*, or "funeral offering," the son *feeds* the father's shade, and in a way the father giving his mortal substance to the son at the moment of death is also a sort of feeding. In one text, the dying father is instructed to place himself upon his son's body, touching the son's organs with his own, and to place each of his vital functions into the son; these include speech, breath (*prāna*), vision, hearing, locomotion, pleasure and pain, happiness, mind, wisdom, etc.

The theory seems to be that the mortal substance of the father passes to his son, and then returns to the father via the son as immortal substance. The process is essentially the same as a sacrifice, or later Hindu offering to the gods (*pūja*), where ordinary, mortal substance (food) returns to the worshipper as divine substance. In other terms, what goes dead into the sacrifice returns as new life. By giving himself (sacrificing himself) to the son, the father is reborn in heaven.

The bad father who will not make this sacrifice and would "eat" the son, literally and prematurely, is appropriately punished in our story: Hariścandra's belly swells with dropsy (an image of greed?) and Ajīgarta loses religious status, being compared to a Śudra. The effect on the son is either to deprive him of bodily and social selfhood (as would happen to Rohita or Śunahśepa if they agreed to be killed for their father's sakes), or to force him to rebel and so lose the father–son relationship entirely.

In "Śunahśepa," Rohita takes the second alternative and opts out of the sacrifice; he severs ties with the patrilineage and becomes a forest wanderer. As such, he is an uninitiated male, with the social status of an outcaste. In the woods, however, he meets the god Indra who teaches him the value of solitary wandering. During his five years as Indra's student, Rohita matures and is initiated by the god; finally he becomes ready to resolve the impasse with his father.

The boy Śunahśepa, whom Rohita purchases from the bad father Ajīgarta, is apparently Rohita's alter ego. With him, Rohita begins to develop the discriminating consciousness that can separate the "good" father image in his experience of Hariścandra from the "bad" one, while not splitting the two sides completely. As a result, Rohita can assist Hariścandra's initiation and development into an integrated – but generally "good" – father. Perhaps – as may be suggested by his name – Śunahśepa (Dog's Tail) is initially a "bad self" image whom Rohita intends to sacrifice to the bad father part of Hariścandra, possibly represented by the god Varuna (a baleful figure somewhat resembling Saturn). Rohita intends to ransom himself with Śunahśepa, and thus sacrifice part of himself to the father while retaining a separate part which will not be sacrificed. The effect seems to be to limit or reject the illegitimate demands of the bad father while performing the spiritual self-enhancing role required by the good, initiated father.

Viśvamitra, the sage who represents the good father, suggests something of this necessary self-enhancement in his praise of his younger sons who accept Śunahśepa-Devāarata as their elder. He says that they have made him "rich in offspring." Obviously it is not a question of numbers; Viśvamitra already has one hundred sons. The sense seems rather that, by communicating with the gods, Śunahśepa has become in some way divine, and that through him, Viśvamitra, too, has forged a bond with the gods, thus enriching his sense of selfhood. His own initiation or individuation is furthered in this way. As a result of Śunahśepa's and Rohita's development, the latter's father, Hariścandra, is released from his bonds. The father-god Varuna is appeased.

Apparently Hariścandra's "badness" has been overcome, and he can be reunited with his still-living son. Ajīgarta and Viśvamitra's older sons remain odd men out and continue to represent untransformed badness; they cannot give the necessary part of themselves to their son and father, respectively, and so remain uninitiated into their true selfhood.

The Śunaḥśepa story, then, is one of adolescents initiated to individuality, discriminating consciousness, and spiritual awareness, and of fathers taught to value the spiritual in their sons and renounce the need to control and depend on them excessively. As the son individuates and forges a relationship with the divine, he communicates some of this to the father, who learns to let go his more primitive need to prolong himself by "eating" the son.

Akanandun likewise seems to undergo a symbolic initiation into discrimination when his head is cut off and his body is articulated into its constituent parts. By giving portions of Akanandun's cooked flesh to each of his relatives, the *sannyasi* apportions the boy according to the claims of his archetypal elements – mother, father, sister, etc. But surprisingly – and this is the critical move of the story – one portion of Akanandun is reserved for the boy himself. It is as if the value of Akanandun's ego is after all recognized, so that over and beyond his collective, archetypal contents there remains a sense of individual selfhood. The boy's death and rebirth is essentially a transformation from preconscious immersion in the psychic life of the family to discrimination of what in himself belongs to the family and what is his alone. Like Śunaḥśepa and Rohita, he learns that he is more than a part of his father (and other family members).

As in "Śunaḥśepa," the lesson in "Akanandun" is as much or more for the parents as the boy; like Hariścandra, they are taught that there is a part of their son which is not theirs. They are shown in an excruciating way – particularly so for vegetarian Brahmans! – the dark side of their need for Akanandun. In being forced to eat him, it is as if their narcissistic dependency on their son is shoved down their throats; they are forced to see its polluted, unclean side. All twelve-year-olds must be sacrificed by their parents, as they grow gradually away from the family; because Akanandun is so wonderful, because each family member has so much sense of self riding on him, his family has an especially hard time letting go. In Maurice Sendak's modern fairy tale, *Where the Wild Things Are*, the wild things (which seem to represent the darker instinctual side of the boy Max and his parents) don't want to let the boy go away, and say, "We'll eat you up we love you so." Even for wild things this would have been a bitter meal; how much more so for Akanandun's doting family.

As suggested earlier, Akanandun's sacrifice and eating by his family is a *pūja*; while it has characteristics of a black mass, or an inverted *pūja* where the food is cursed rather than blessed, in the end all is well and we may take the offering as positive. Precisely because a share is reserved for Akanandun himself, and his individual selfhood is preserved, the nourishment each parent and sister receives from him can be understood as a *transformed*, spiritual essence of Akanandun, which can now be given and received without violating the boy's selfhood. The adolescent becomes his own person and the mid-life parents learn not to depend literally, at the level of the narcissistic ego, on their son.

Both our stories, then, refer to adolescence and mid-life, and to the relationship between the transformation of the child (son) and parent (father). The spiritual nature of this transformation can be made clearer by referring to another ancient fairy tale from the same period as "Śunahśepa," the famous story of Naciketas and Death from the *Katha Upanishad* (see De Vries 1987). Like Rohita and Akanandun, Naciketas is sacrificed by his father, who like Rohita's father is at a stage of personal crisis and as a result acts like a "bad" father.

Naciketas

Naciketas's father Vajaśravasa is ritually consecrated for the *sarvavedas* (All Possessions) sacrifice. Naciketas asks, "To whom will you give me?" His father replies, "I give you to Death!" Naciketas arrives at Death's house, but Death is absent and fails to provide hospitality. When Death returns after three days, he makes amends for his *faux pas* by giving Naciketas three wishes.

With his first wish Naciketas asks to be returned to an even-minded father whose anger is gone and whose anxieties are pacified. Death grants this, and says that the father will henceforth sleep peacefully through the night.

Naciketas then asks to learn the sacrifice that leads to heaven, and Death grants this and names it after Naciketas. The third wish is the essence of the matter, however: Naciketas asks the secret of death, whether a man is or is not after death. Death offers a number of tempting substitutes, but Naciketas persists in his question. Finally Death instructs Naciketas in the *ātmavidya*, the paradoxical nature of the true Self which is not born and does not die, which acts without acting, goes everywhere without moving, rejoices and yet does not rejoice. Finally Naciketas returns to his father.

Although the Naciketas story does not, like "Śunaḥśepa" and "Akanandun," explicitly involve the reverse prestation of a son to the gods via sacrifice, Death is certainly a god, and it is as a result of sacrifice (literally a "total prestation") that he is sent to Death's kingdom. As Naciketas tells Death, there is much question among men about the mortal condition after death, and the point of his journey to Death is to find out the answer to this question. It does not seem too farfetched to suggest that the issue is on his father's mind as well and might even be the motivation for his sacrifice. That it is an "all possessions" sacrifice suggests death, since at death all one's possessions are given away, including the vital faculties. It is also significant that Naciketas's first wish involves pacifying his father's anxieties and helping him to sleep at night. Vajaśravasa, then, may have been caught in a mid-life depression, afraid and unsure in the face of death. Like a "bad" Indian father, he sends his son to die in his place, but like Rohita, and implicitly Akanandun, the youth finds the spiritual realization that saves the father as well as himself.

Our stories are, in part, examples of the "old king" category, where the fresh and naive energies of youth are needed to renew the old man, but in a way contrary to the old man's tendency to hoard and hold onto the dregs of his own youth until the bitter end. Unlike many Western instances of the "old king" theme, however, renewal does not necessarily involve the death of the old man and his literal replacement by a young one. Rather, in order to let go of his son, and his own hold on youth, the aging father needs to be initiated into the mysteries of a Self beyond death. The crisis of adolescence, with its intense concerns over selfhood and mortality, can bring illumination to the mid-life crisis and its similar concerns. One is reminded of the twelve-year-old Jesus confounding the elders in the temple, or of Śiva as Eternal Youth (*Sanāt-kumāra*) instructing the grey-bearded Brahmans under the bodhi tree.

Because Naciketas (whose name De Vries suggests may mean "Ignorant") has the open mind of a "Dummling," he is ready to confront Death without fear and to take advantage of his one-up position when Death fails the duties of a proper host. Because he is clear about what he wants and not paralyzed with anxiety, he is a fit vessel for the profound secret of the Self which Death imparts. Naciketas reminds one of Percival in the Grail castle, but a Percival who does not forget to ask.

Suggested but left somewhat unclear in the three tales so far considered is the nature of the bad father's pathology. He is clearly afraid of death and the loss of his own powers (including the son who incarnates his powers and whom he refuses to let grow up and away from him). In "Śunahśepa" he is also starving, and the oral theme is central in "Akanandun" as well. Another contemporary fairy tale – one with roots in the ancient tradition – will deepen our understanding of the father's problems with nurturance, and with the nurturing Mother.

The Wicked Mendicant
(folktale collected in contemporary India)

O nce upon a time there was a king who had seven queens. But still he had no peace of mind because he had no children. Because of his inauspicious condition, the king one day shut himself up in his chamber and resolved to put an end to his own life.

Soon a mendicant [*sannyasi*] came to the palace and asked to see the king. The king came out of his chamber and received the holy ascetic with great respect. The mendicant gave the king the root of a particular plant and told him to grind it into a powder and distribute the powder to each of his queens. If this was done, he assured the king, his queens would conceive. However, he made it a condition of the conception that the best of the king's children must later be given to him. The king agreed. The root was ground into a powder and given to the seven queens. But the six older queens took all of the powder for themselves and wouldn't let the youngest have any. So, the youngest queen took some water and washed the stone on which the root was ground. She then drank the water.

In due course, the queens all gave birth. The sons of the six elder queens were born with defective limbs, while the youngest gave birth to a conch shell. Seeing this, the king drove his youngest queen away from the palace. At night she began to dream that a beautiful baby had come out of the conch shell each evening and suckled at her breast. One night she only pretended to be asleep and saw a real baby emerge from the conch shell and begin to suck at her breast. The child told his mother that an evil *sannyasi* wanted to take him away and that this was his reason for hiding in the shell. The mother assured the child that this could not happen, and together they returned to the palace. Seeing the beautiful male child in the queen's lap, the king realized his mistake and received her back with great respect. When this prince reached the age of twelve, the mendicant returned and demanded that the king give up his best son. The king could not refuse. The miserable queen was told by some neighboring women to worship the goddess Sankata Mangal Chandi as her only chance of getting her son back. The queen did this.

The mendicant, accompanied by the young prince, now entered a dense forest. After some time, they reached a temple of the fierce goddess Kāli. The mendicant asked the prince to take his daily bath in the temple tank. As he did so, he was horrified to find a huge heap of human skulls which laughed as he stared.

The skulls told the boy, "We are laughing at the thought that one more skull will be added to our pile today. We were brought here by the mendicant in the same way that you have been. All of us have been sacrificed to the goddess. Today it is your turn. There is only one way you can avoid this fate, but it is difficult." The skulls told him that at the end of his worship, the mendicant would ask the boy to bow down in front of the idol of the goddess. They advised him to ask the mendicant to show him the proper way to bow at that moment since, as the son of a king, he had never had to bow before. When the mendicant demonstrated how to bow, the prince was to take the sword from the hand of the idol and behead the mendicant with a single stroke. He should then sprinkle the man's blood on all the skulls. In this way they would all be brought back to life.

The prince carried out the plan and ended the life of the wicked mendicant. The skulls were revived and they, as well as the young prince, returned to their respective countries. The parents of each missing child were delighted.

While this tale is complicated, and seems to be told from several points of view, there are clear parallels to the stories we are treating. First and most obvious, a son must be returned at age twelve to the *sannyasi* – and ultimately to the divinity – who gave him to a childless king. In this tale, however, the *sannyasi* functions as the bad father who will not let go his son (similar to the god Varuṇa in "Śunaḥśepa"). The "root" that inseminates the queen comes from him, and the story's end suggests that the *sannyasi* has used the life blood of the children to prolong his own life: hence when he dies, and his blood is returned to the youths' skulls, they come back to life.

Our story shares many elements with the title story of Heinrich Zimmer's book, *The King and the Corpse*, where an evil magician tries to sacrifice a young man to the goddess Kāli, but has the tables turned on him and becomes himself the victim of the sacrifice. As here, an evil father figure and *guru* is caught in the dark side of the Great Mother, to whom he must sacrifice others in order to save himself. It seems that a father who cannot let go his sons may have regressed to a state of partial fusion with the devouring Mother, into whose maw he throws his sons so that she will not eat him.

It seems significant that in all of our stories except "Naciketas," the father initially suffers from a surfeit of the feminine: one hundred wives in "Śunaḥśepa," seven daughters in "Akanandun," seven queens in "The Wicked Mendicant." The Indian male's traditional way out of the Mother and her female hordes is through the patrilineage, the masculine staircase that leads through the father, grandfather, and great grandfather all the way to the gods. The bad father, however, cannot find this "broad, well-trodden road where those who have sons walk free from sorrow," as Narada's *gātha*-s have it. Instead he "eats" his sons, or psychologically is possessed by the devouring Mother who eats them with his mouth.

"Akanandun" shows the true path by having the son be eaten not only by father (and also mother and sisters), but *by himself* as well. Only through fathers giving the self-substance they share with their sons back to their sons can their patrilineage be extended onward into the future. When the hero of "The Wicked Mendicant" pours the *sannyasi*'s blood on the children's skulls, in effect he feeds the father's blood – acquired by cannibalistically devouring the sons – back to the sons. In another way, the eater is himself eaten in this story: the mendicant beheaded with the goddess's sword can be seen as eaten by her. It is as if the mother complex is fed to the archetype that underlies it, with the result that both sons and the good father are released from thrall to the devouring goddess. Apparently the good-mother side of the goddess (Sankata Mangal Chandi) is integrated into the father–son relationship, so that each can "feed" the other in an appropriate way.

The theme of the "barren father," which is present in three of our stories, is a very common and important one in Indian culture. While it is obvious that the Indian father requires a son to carry on his self, we are now in a position to see that the sonless father may be so primarily because he unconsciously does not *want* a son and fears the loss of self which a son represents. The "sins" that Akanandun's father committed in a past life might have been directed against a former son, and the king in "The Wicked Mendicant" banishes his conch-shell son to the forest. Moreover, the son sacrifice that these fathers are required to make is consonant with the side of their ambivalence which would hold fast to their egoic, "body–mind self" (Kohut 1977) and refuse the *self*-sacrifice a son entails. The resulting spiritual hunger – like being gnawed by the goddess Kāli – can, paradoxically, only be assuaged by the son they fear.

CONCLUSION

Our stories involve the age-appropriate sacrifice of the masculine ego, father's and son's, and its transformation through spiritual initiation. Although the son begins the process, both participants realize, beyond – and *through* – the inherence of their physical and social selfhood in one another, the reality of a Self transcending both of them which also reaches the "far shore" of personal, or ego, death.

The old king is renewed psychologically by a son who refuses to do so literally or physically, but who is open to the gods and – shamanlike – can carry back their wisdom to his father. Some old kings are beyond redemption and, like Ajīgarta and the wicked mendicant, are rejected or killed. Likewise some sons are interested only in the ego and its possessions and cannot honor the gods. But fathers and sons – the masculine at adolescence and mid-life – are caught in similar crises of individuation and must sacrifice their childish tendency to regress back to Mother. The main realization we take from these stories is that father and son – despite their natural conflicts – can help each other in this letting go and can find a way to feed one another spiritually that is not a regression.

REFERENCES

"Śunaḥśepa" is from the *Aitareya Brāhmaṇa* (7.14–17; Haug, 1863); "Naciketas" frames the entire *Katha Upaniṣhad* (Radhakrishnan, 1953). Each has been translated and condensed by A. Collins. "Akanandun" and "The Wicked Mendicant" are paraphrased from Beck *et al.* (1987).

Beck, B. E. F., Claus, P. J., Goswami, P., and Handoo, J. 1987. *Folktales of India*. Chicago: University of Chicago Press.

DeVries, L. 1987. The father, the son and the ghoulish host: a fairy tail in ancient Sanskrit? *Asian Folklore Studies* 46:227–256.

Haug, M., ed. 1863. *Aitareya Brāhmaṇa*. Bombay: Government Central Book Depot.

Kohut, H. 1977. *The Restoration of the Self*. New York: International Universities Press.

Radhakrishnan, S. 1953. *The Principal Upanishads*. London: Allen and Unwin.

Ramanujan, A. K. 1983. The Indian Oedipus. In *Oedipus: A Folklore Casebook*, L. Edmunds and A. Dundes, eds. New York: Garland, pp. 234–261.

Sendak, M. 1963. *Where the Wild Things Are*. New York: Harper and Row.

Zimmer, H. 1971. *The King and the Corpse*. Princeton, N.J.: Princeton University Press.

"The Water of Life"
A Story of Healing and the Transformation of Consciousness

David L. Hart

Because fairy tales deal in the extremities of life, there is a widespread feeling that they are uncanny or spooky. By facing into the supernatural, they totally relativize our accepted world of experience, giving it a weird, unheard-of dimension. And yet it is just this new dimension that allows us to see that there is no extremity of life, however dire, that does not offer a way out. The threat of death, which is standard fare in fairy tales, leaps up to confront us in order to show, ultimately and finally, what *life* is. We begin to see that "death" and "life" may not be quite what we had thought. Perhaps they are qualities of our living experience, the fairy tale then being a guide to the way that leads to life. If this is so, it is clear that we are dealing with something very different from physical life and death.

Fairy tales are certainly instructive in the broadest possible sense, but I do not feel that they can be explained away on that ground – for instance, as moral or social instruction, illustrating that virtue is rewarded and vice punished. They reflect rather the acute, living confrontation between the human world and another world which it is difficult not to call the divine. Although it is true that this other world is frequently weird, we shall see from our present tale that this weirdness is really our own reaction, and that the supernatural proves to have ultimate power and life.

It can even be said that fairy tales often seem to carry the hidden thread of a spiritual understanding whose efficacy has been lost in the official religious life. Thus spiritual healing, a vital part of Jesus' ministry, certainly got buried in Christianity, at least until recently; yet many great tales, such as our story, "The Water of Life," convey just this message of the healing power of the divine. The restoration and healing which occur in them are explicitly not through mere material means, but are effected through a marvelous, elusive substance only obtained by absolute proof of the spiritual qualifications of the one who seeks it. This means, psychologically, that it is our mental orientation that will determine how we fare in our quest for redemption and spiritual deliverance.

The present story happens to illustrate this point in a very striking way. As we read it, it is important to try to think of the different characters as distinct, possible tendencies in our own thinking and reacting. That way we can make this story our own in surprising ways. Thus, rather than objectifying the characters too much, we can say, "How does that one illustrate me or my experience?" And: "What are the consequences of that fact?"

"The Water of Life" is in the complete *Grimm's Fairy Tales*, one of those stories originally collected from the German folk tradition by the Brothers Grimm.

The Water of Life

There was once a king who was so ill that no one believed he would survive. He had three sons who were extremely upset about it and who went down into the palace garden and wept. There they met an old man who asked them why they were so sad. They told him about their father, and that nothing seemed to cure him. He replied, "I know of one more remedy, and that is the water of life; if he drinks of it, he will become well again; but it is hard to find."

The eldest son went to the king and begged to be allowed to go for the water which would heal him. The king said, "No, the danger of it is too great. I would rather die." But his son begged until the king consented. The son thought, "If I bring the water, then I shall be best beloved of my father, and shall inherit the kingdom."

He set out on his horse and soon met a dwarf, who asked, "Whither away so fast?" The young man said, "Silly shrimp, it is nothing to do with you," and rode on. But the angry dwarf wished him an evil wish, and soon the eldest son rode between two mountains that grew ever closer until he was totally stuck between them. As he did not return, the second son, with the same ambition to inherit, persuaded his father to let him go. He met exactly the same fate as the eldest. So it goes with haughty people.

The youngest son persuaded his father to let him go. When the dwarf questioned his haste, he stopped and said, "I am seeking the water of life, for my father is sick unto death." The dwarf rewarded his good behavior with the information that the water of life was in the courtyard of an enchanted castle; but to enter the iron door he must strike three times with an iron wand, and he must feed two hungry lions with two loaves of bread. Then he must fetch the water and leave the castle by twelve or be imprisoned there.

All went as the dwarf had said. Within the castle were enchanted princes whose rings he took from their fingers; a sword and a loaf of bread he took with him; and a beautiful maiden who kissed him and said he had set her free and could marry her if he returned in a year, but warned him to get out with the water before twelve. But the prince lay down wearily on a beautifully made bed, fell asleep, and woke at quarter to twelve. In a fright, he fetched a cup of the water of life and barely made it out of the iron door, which cut off a piece of his heel as it clanged shut.

The prince, rejoicing at having the water, met the dwarf again, who told him that the sword he now had could slay whole armies and the bread would never be used up. The young man begged the dwarf to release his brothers from their imprisonment; the dwarf did so with the warning that they had bad hearts. But the youngest son told them all about the water of life and everything else.

As they traveled home, he loaned his sword and his bread to the kings of three different kingdoms devastated by war and famine, so that all of them achieved peace and plenty. Then, as the three brothers went over the sea and the youngest slept, the two eldest plotted and stole the water of life from him, putting salt seawater into his cup instead.

When they got home, the salt water brought by the youngest made the king sicker than ever; upon which the elder brothers gave the king the water of life, and he recovered his health. They warned the youngest son to say nothing, and the king, thinking the latter had plotted to kill him, grew angry, sentenced him to death, and ordered a huntsman to take him into the forest and shoot him.

Once in the forest, the huntsman could not carry out the sentence and confessed all to the prince, who was shocked. The prince begged the huntsman to change clothes with him and then went further into the forest while the huntsman returned home. After a time, three wagon-loads of gold and precious stones came to the king, sent by the three kings whose kingdoms had been saved by the sword and bread of the youngest son. The king began to wonder, "Can my son have been innocent?" and openly admitted his grief that he had had him killed. Then the huntsman told him the truth, and a stone fell from the king's heart. He let it be known that the prince was in favor and might return home.

Meanwhile, the princess had a bright golden road made leading up to her palace and gave instructions that only the person who rode straight up it would be the right one, and not any one riding alongside it. The year was now nearly up, so the eldest son thought he would go to claim her as her savior, and the kingdom as well. So he rode in haste, but when he saw the road, he thought, "It would be a sin and a shame if I were to ride over that," and went along the right side. At the palace, he was turned away. The second prince set out and, likewise fearing to damage the road, rode on the left side, with the same result.

But now, as the year was entirely up, the third son rode out from the forest toward the palace. He yearned so incessantly for the princess, with whom he could forget his sorrows, that he never noticed the golden road at all and rode right up the middle of it. So he was welcomed as her savior and lord of the kingdom, and they were married. She told him his father had forgiven him, and he went home, and told the old king how his brothers had betrayed him and yet he had kept silent. The father wanted to punish them, but they had put to sea, never to return.

The opening of this story reveals a lone king, without wife or consort, and so ill that apparently all known remedies have failed to help him, and therefore he is expected to die. Whatever he has, it is not accessible to the ministrations of the familiar material world. Because it is beyond the competence of this world, it is the cause of despair for the king's three sons.

This is a common motif: extreme despair that leads to weeping turns up at critical points in many fairy tales. When it is the king who is sick unto death, we have a crisis of the central meaning and authority of life, which radiates into every other part of it. In psychological terms, the king is the principle which governs one's actions and mind, and it is this principle that is shown to be in mortal decline.

The first really positive reaction to this crisis – although it may not seem so – is the utter desperation of the three sons. They represent all the new life and hope in this royal family, and their total concentration on the crisis actually calls forth a wholly unexpected response. As we admit our helplessness and therewith implicitly throw ourselves on something unknown, that unknown will come to meet us. Here, an unanticipated old man stands in the garden in response to the admission of despair and need.

He makes them state the problem – the sickness of their father. This is important in view of the confrontation that will occur later to each of the three sons on the road. Fairy tales generally follow this form: the helpful one asks what the matter is, and the hero or heroine has to lay it out in words before help becomes possible. This admission is an essential element of progress toward a solution, just as it is, for instance, in psychotherapy, where openness about the problem is absolutely essential and is often, mysteriously, a part of the solution itself.

Once the problem is put out there, an answer is forthcoming. The "water of life" is an extraordinary name, highly suggestive of the water Jesus differentiated from the material, common water: the "living water" of which he said, "Whosoever drinketh of the water that I shall give him shall never thirst; but the water that I shall give him shall be in him a well of water springing up into everlasting life" (John 4:13, 14).

The eldest son, the first impulse to seek and find the water of life, represents our first and most accessible kind of reaction to need, namely our attitude that also seeks its own perpetuation and security. "If I bring the water, then I shall be best beloved of my father, and shall inherit the kingdom." The quest becomes an opportunity for self-aggrandizement. Much of our modern emphasis on psychological "growth" has just this kind of security in mind, that of being "first in the kingdom," "best beloved," and so on.

It is interesting that his father, the king, tries to prevent his going, saying, "No, the danger of it is too great. I would rather die." There is an intuition here that if this quest is undertaken, things are never going to be the same again, and to perish on familiar ground seems preferable. This is the basis for the resistance to real change that occurs at critical points in development: one of the reactions is that death would really be better than the total uncertainty of something new and untried.

Now comes, for the first son, the crucial confrontation of his quest. Fairy tales often contain tests of this kind, and they are usually not merely a matter of passing or failing, but of life or death. So it is here, for the life of the king hangs on the success of his sons.

The first son has scarcely begun his journey when he encounters the dwarf and incurs his anger. The dwarf, who proves to hold the key to any further advance of these heroes, seems like a new version of the old man in the garden. But being a dwarf, he also represents the prejudice and distortion visited on a source of wisdom that has been rejected by the conscious world. True to their limited values, the two elder sons carry forward this prejudice, trusting only in their own preconceived notions of the way and rejecting their unlikely would-be helper. So it is that our illusion of wisdom – represented here by two brothers, that is, by a doubleness or duality of vision – goes charging off in arrogant haste, egocentric and superior.

Both of the brothers wind up imprisoned between two mountains. We were told how their motivation was secretly tainted by their craving for self-aggrandizement. This craving exists in conflict with their genuine concern for their father: it means that they are literally of two minds, divided, ambivalent. The direct result of such ambivalence of motive is a paralysis between two demands that eventually leaves no room to act at all. The imprisonment of the older sons is the inevitable consequence of their dividedness and of the fact that they cannot admit it and therewith get straight with the world. Whatever the water of life is, it is not to be sought with the usual worldly, dualistic mind.

In the story, this represents a period of great pain and frustration, as hope dies for the first brave attempts to achieve healing. Absolutely nothing comes back from them, so these seemingly most reliable functions, the elder sons, have proved bankrupt. In other words, the mind and its energies have exhausted themselves: all of its cleverness avails nothing.

It is important to see that the third son, who is of a very different essence, emerges only after and out of this frustration of the other two. It is clear that genuine renewal and healing involves some part of ourselves that is not immediately obvious in our "normal" way of thinking and perceiving – not what we trust right off the bat, but rather a last resort when all else has failed. But what really has to fail seems to be self-will and pride, the arrogance that takes all to oneself ("The kingdom will fall to me").

It is the failure that makes room for the youngest son, in whom are none of those qualities. He is accosted by the dwarf exactly as were his brothers, but his reaction is different. His brothers continued in their haste, whereas he is stopped by the question, that is, a compulsive or automatic movement is finally brought to a halt. Haste indicates something frantic and betrays fear, and sure enough, those who were subject to it really did not know where they were going. That whole state of mind is now halted. The third son is a faculty for listening, asking, and relating, and is essentially without fear.

He also is without the obvious double-mindedness of his brothers. The only concern he seems to have is the one he tells about. "I am seeking the water of life, for my father is sick unto death." He is thinking of the ultimate, not of himself. And as it is where one's thought is that determines where oneself is, his thought puts him immediately in touch with his goal.

He still needs the dwarf, however, because certain essential attitudes are presented to him in order to succeed in his quest. First, the water of life springs from a fountain in the courtyard of an enchanted castle, indicating that it is under a spell. This common motif of fairy tales signifies the realm of that which has not yet been awakened, brought into life, and made real. The water of life lies in a place still dormant, still shut off from the conscious world.

Second, it is perceived as a place that can only be entered in a special way, that is, if the hero strikes three times with an iron wand on the iron door of the castle, after which it will spring open. The bringing of iron to iron, that is, meeting the new world with its own substance, is a common motif and signifies the submergence of his own will and the isolated thinking of which this hero is capable, putting him in genuine harmony with what he meets.

And finally, this enchanted world is perceived as perilous: two gaping lions guard the entrance. The third son is supplied with bread to still these frightening beasts. The lions embody that fear of the new and untried which led the old king to refuse help in the first place: images of fear regularly arise at such junctures, for instance, in therapy when a whole new direction is being undertaken and something in us says, "Oh no! I can't do that!"

The hero with the bread is our means of stilling that fear, therewith giving it the lie. The new way was not inaccessible after all, and it would have been fatal to trust our first reactions.

Thus the so-called inaccessible, or the "treasure hard to obtain," becomes accessible; in fact, the hero makes an unexpected discovery. There is a large and splendid hall and there are enchanted princes whose rings he removes from their fingers, apparently signifying their release from bewitchment. There is, in short, great wealth and great potential energy for life locked away in this secret place, now being opened up to consciousness. An inexhaustible wealth seems often to characterize the enchanted world when its enchantment is broken into; it is that source of life that is experienced as boundlessly healing, of which I spoke at the beginning. It is in this place, too, that the hero finds the sword and loaf of bread whose power will prove itself later on.

The prize of prizes, however, is the princess herself, who is filled with joy and gratitude when she sees the prince. Why? He has "set her free." That means his very presence in this castle is itself liberation. All consciousness has to do is be there, and the immense shutdown of life, which fairy tales depict as bewitchment, is overcome: life is released joyfully to itself.

The words *bewitchment*, and especially *enchantment*, are often used in a highly positive sense. It is interesting, however, that not only fairy tales but also individuals seeking to grow frequently register bewitchment as an unknowing, frozen, even dangerous state, preferring instead whatever reality lies beyond this state. The release from bewitchment means that a certain compulsion and slavishness are over, and that one is seeing and being seen for oneself and not according to a projected image, however glamorous. It is, in our story, the difference between knowing the princess and being content with legends about a remote, perilous castle. The truth of our being wants to be known as does the princess here, and she signifies both "anima" or soul in Jung's sense and the soul of another—as the great work of the fairy tale embraces both inner and outer worlds.

Now the princess sets a term upon the final union between herself and the hero, promising both her kingdom and herself if he will return to her in a year. Why? He has obviously not won her yet. A year is a complete cycle of time, after which the reunion will occur at the same time yet on a new level. What she is telling him is that, if he is really to win her, he has to pass through something more first. She sets conditions whose real meaning will only unfold in the future. She has in her secret mind knowledge of what is really required before a final integration can take place, that mystical union of inner and outer that Jung calls the experience of the Self.

It is important to note that such a story never ends right at this point, as if the mere coming together of hero and heroine were all that was required. But at this point a wish or illusion of fulfillment can beguile consciousness into taking a long rest. The third son is seduced into taking a nap on a fresh beautiful bed, narrowly avoiding becoming trapped in this place for good. Here we have a true mortal danger, that of the illusion of fulfillment and of a permanent solution or of permanent peace, a trap into which seekers really can fall, forever afterward ignoring the world and the great problem of reconciling to it the newly gained treasure and insight. Our hero nearly falls into this trap in spite of two explicit warnings to get the water of life out of there before twelve.

One recalls that Cinderella likewise underwent considerable metamorphosis at the hour of twelve, the hour at which the glamour is over and the hard, worldly work begins of reconciling the old and the new: in Cinderella's case, the long, hard search of the prince for Cinderella in the most unlikely place; and in our case, the long, hard trial and proof of the third son against apparently overwhelming odds. But just as the prince's vision of Cinderella impels him onward to the goal, so the real treasures now in the third son's hands will both sustain and justify him in the end.

What he has to encounter, in short, is the old mind, or what St. Paul calls the "old man" in all its forms. How does truth, life, spiritual reality possibly make it with all our old, habitual reactions and ways of thinking and feeling? How can truth and illusion mix? How can we actually live and embody a truth we have inwardly glimpsed and in some sense made our own? And what will that do to our whole lifestyle, place in the world, and even identity? Out of these questions and the reactions they produce, the next events of this story become comprehensible.

There is, first of all, an unmistakable joy within the prince, that he has obtained and carries the water of life. This deep joy can be felt, whatever our circumstances, when the transforming and healing work is under way. The water of life, that indescribable substance, brings with it life and joy, and as we shall see, spreads its effect even when its true source is not properly acknowledged. Beyond the water, there are the sword and loaf of bread, which, at this point in the story, the dwarf pronounces to be "great wealth."

The nature of the third son is nowhere more openly revealed than in his attitude toward his older brothers, who have remained stuck between the two mountains, totally out of the picture that has been unfolding. The youngest begs the dwarf to release them, and when he does, tells them his whole story without any guile or holding back. It is in his nature to be whole, inclusive, and single in his approach to all things, so much so, indeed, that he does not see betrayal even when it is staring him in the face, even when he has been warned about it. The wounding of his heel gives him the mark of some mortal weakness or temptation, yet his trust of life is really extraordinary and carries him finally to a very high demonstration of ultimate reality. It is because he is willing and able to embrace all, good and bad, that he can also pass a test that takes him through all of it, so that the transformation depicted in this story represents great spiritual achievement. Like that of many fairy tales, it is offered as a picture of the possibility of our development—certainly not just a wish fulfillment to make us feel better, but a signpost to what really can make us better, to what really can heal.

The fidelity of the youngest son has led to deep healing effects that already show themselves even as the three brothers travel homeward. They encounter three separate kingdoms in all of which war and famine are ravaging the countryside. With his sword, the youngest son can ensure the end of war, and with his bread the end of famine. These three unredeemed kingdoms, so typical of fairy tales, portray that chronic untreated state of deprivation and conflict from which we suffer inwardly until healing occurs. They point out the stupendous loss of energy that arises from this state, so meaningless in itself, and how the cure is simply in eliminating it, not in "finding a solution." For this is, in fact, a state of mind, locked in on itself in endless waste, and only the intrusion from without of a whole new spirit will bring it to an end. Jung has supported the same point of view in showing that if you pursue the questions of ultimate importance, symptoms will regularly disappear in time, as a "side-effect." Thus the hero, pursuing the ultimate, has healed an apparently incurable state in the process.

There follows a sea journey of the three brothers, which represents the actual point of transition at which the new and the old begin to clash: the new life encountering the old mind. The older brothers are reactivated and taking control; that is, the habitual, dualistic, ego-centered mind wants to take credit for this unheard-of, marvelous substance which has somehow been brought back into its world. Thus we are tempted to claim credit for life itself, not acknowledging that it is solely a gift from a source we cannot really fathom or comprehend; thus we want to say, "Look what I did." The brothers are aware that their own security is in jeopardy ("our father will give him the kingdom which belongs to us") if they let the youngest take credit; so tenacious is the self-maintaining impulse of this ego-based mind, which is of all our functions the most resistant to fundamental change.

They exchange the water of life for salt sea-water which they place with their brother, leaving him to bring it to the sick king. The sleep of the youngest brother represents an eclipse of truth typical of this stage, at which the old mind seizes on the real substance and uses it for its own purposes. Meanwhile the new mind conveys something quite unpalatable and apparently even more harmful than the original problem. This is an interesting commentary on the way in which new truth typically comes to first realization. It may seem very hard to stomach and may taste terrible, so that the imagery of salt water is quite apt. When King Lear's third daughter Cordelia compared him to salt, where the older daughters had flattered him by comparing him to things of great material value, this too "tasted" awful and led Lear to banish his only loyal child.

It seems that the healing spirit has to sneak in to do its work via the older and more familiar paths of the mind, which will reassure the king, tempting him to believe that all is still in order and that no further transformation is in the works. This stage is one at which renewal has been accepted with absolutely no concern about its source. It is an unconscious living out of the healing event, complacently assuming it to be one's own achievement and pretty much a proof that one is, after all, great: the king is in his supreme place, and this place is well supported by his two older sons, who are an extension of himself.

Why is the youngest son, meanwhile, not permitted, on pain of death, to speak a word in his own behalf? His older brothers grant him his life only if he will refrain from revealing their plot, that is, only if he will take on himself the presumption of guilt — as if he really intended to poison his father. The true hero or heroine committed to total silence in the face of criminal accusations is not uncommon in fairy tales. It seems monstrously unfair that this hero should suffer conviction and even a death sentence in total innocence while the true culprits ride high.

The point of this painful development is that space and time must be created for a total inner purging of all that stands in the way of the truth. It is not a question of one person's word against another's, the third son's word against his brothers'. This would put the story on the level of ordinary human retribution and justification. The lack of this kind of justification in such a story makes room for a "change of mind," or *metanoia*, in which these human motivations are no longer the point. By his silence, the hero is saying, in effect, that reality is altogether different from such issues as who is right and who is wrong, who is up and who is down, who is in and who is out – all the standards by which our ordinary human minds are prone to judge and direct our lives.

"The Water of Life" is a profound spiritual story. It is true to a reality quite beyond that of the "known" world, yet accessible to our spiritual awareness and capable of informing and confirming it. The person of the third son stands like a guide to possibilities of insight and final reconciliation of our different worlds, in that at every point we find him holding out for the whole, the ultimate – especially in contrast to the hasty and partial orientation characteristic of his brothers.

The old king, his father, represents the overall orientation of consciousness, our view of life; hence the vital importance of the change that must take place in him. At this moment he continues under the illusion of the old mental structure, dominated by the limited, self-serving view of his older sons, and therefore necessarily suppressing and repressing that vision of totality embodied in his youngest. The two pictures of life are fundamentally incompatible in the mind. To achieve some sense of unity, therefore, one of them must go, and it is the youngest son who is ordered shot. It is the king's conviction that the renewal offered by his third son would mean his own end – as we may feel that if we let transformation really have its way with us, it will be the end of our "self" as we know it. Better to take the benefit of the water and forget about the wider implications; this is what the king is trying to do.

What actually happens, of course, is that the king's son remains alive but in a changed form. He takes on the clothing of the huntsman, and therewith the prince is reduced to (as he calls it) "common" stature and disappears even further into the forest. The insight and life that he represents retreats far from consciousness; it is no longer considered of any importance; but at the same time, it cannot be killed off. One of the most encouraging facts of spiritual and psychological life is that whatever is real also endures. It is never too late to turn or return to that which is real and makes whole, since it is there somewhere – possibly disguised by repression, but unmistakably there. This story illustrates that it is by our own decision that such contents are lost to consciousness, not by virtue of any "malice" on its part; correspondingly, it harbors no grudge and offers no resistance to being taken up again. There is a great deal to learn from these facts about the third son, who represents not only one's own deepest inner truth but also that of others. We have here a guide both to ourselves and to our relationships, correcting the misapprehension that we are at the mercy of any arbitrary conscious decisions and reactions. Our real life is quite beyond these things.

During this year of the youngest son's trial and proof, these facts begin to dawn on the king himself. Decisive is the fact that three wagonloads of wealth arrive, intended for his youngest son and sent by the three kingdoms which this son released from war and famine. In other words, overwhelming tangible proof that indeed this one was the bearer of truth arrives. The experience of an unaccountable inner joy and gratitude cause one at last to admit that the quality of life has fundamentally changed. In place of deprivation there is bounty; in place of strife, peace. In this acknowledgment we have to see, like the king, that maybe truth came from another source than the one closest to ourselves. Perhaps we have it all backward: perhaps the "least" was in reality the greatest, and the last first. What a tragedy, then, to have snuffed out the life of that one!

So it is that one can lament what seems an irreparable wrong turning in the road, as if the life of the soul had forever been stilled. This lament is possible because meanwhile the "older brothers," that is, our shallower selves, hold sway over the mind, depressing it by their limitations and cynicism. At this point one may say, "If only. . .," as though (and this is the most cynical idea of all) a final decision had been made against real life. In both the therapy of others and one's own inner work comes the despairing words, "It's too late." Since, in a literal sense, this is blatantly untrue, it can only mean: "I have killed off my chances for life, love, and happiness; now I have only a meaningless existence to finish out." By such a point of view, people can maintain themselves pretty much in the meaningless round they have laid out, since, as we keep emphasizing, it is thought that ultimately determines life.

This fairy tale, like almost all fairy tales, is not concerned with the traps along the way except to illuminate them; it wants to bring us beyond them all. Thus a true change of heart can occur in the king at this point when he is told that his youngest son is still alive. More accurately, as the story says, "then a stone fell from the king's heart, and he had it proclaimed in every country that his son might return and be taken into favor again." All this while, in other words, a stone actually lay on the king's heart, as he suffered the secret torture of that dividedness which was the hallmark of his older sons. To be divided is to suffer, even if this suffering is not clearly recognized. To be separated from the source of meaning is torture, no matter how muted and disguised. The king languished in the absence of his true son, and he begins to bloom in the knowledge that his son lives.

There could be no greater demonstration of the indestructibility of what is true and genuine than this story. The third son, as the representative of that genuineness, withstands every assault and innuendo to emerge more genuine than before; and the well-being of the king is proved to rest with him—first by virtue of his healing power, but finally by virtue of the king's own acknowledgment. As fairy tales show in many different ways, the great task of the spiritual life is to arrive at a clear realization of what the source of life really is—that source that, unbeknownst to consciousness, has always sustained it. Only in this realization does true peace become possible.

It now appears that the cycle of this momentous year has been completed, its requirements met, as the king and his youngest son become one in spirit. The seal will be set by another union, that of the redeemed princess with her redeemer. The hero, having proved that no tricks of the mind can do him in, can make permanent and actual his bond with the anima, or soul, who has been released into a living reality. The marriage at the end of fairy tales means a real state of joy and fullness won by devotion to what ultimately matters: not wish-fulfillment but fulfillment—a spiritual state of wholeness and blessedness.

Up to the very end, the elder brothers remain free to try their best to win everything for themselves. They tried, and even succeeded for quite a while, in claiming credit for obtaining the water of life; now that it is time to claim the princess, they are at it again. Each one decides in turn that it is possible and right for him to win her and sets out – typically in haste, for the year has not yet fully expired. Again the compulsiveness that characterized their first attempts to go after the water reveals itself, and when each of them encounters the golden road laid out by the princess, he rides by the side of it. The result is that these suitors are turned away; whereas the third son, his heart dwelling on the princess, comes in the fullness of time not even noticing the road he rides on, with the result that he is recognized as the savior and lord of the princess's kingdom.

In the fairy tale the danger is of undervaluing oneself, but inflation can also be a dangerous pitfall; both are equally fatal states of mind. What they have in common is a narrow ego-centeredness. It is quite apt to speak not only of positive but also of negative inflation, which is the illusion of unworthiness displayed by the two elder brothers. That is the motive that keeps them from riding up the golden road: it is too grand and marvelous for them. A strange turn of events, one might think, after the excessively haughty behavior and lofty attitudes of these two up to now! the last thing you might expect from them would be this abject avoidance of the splendid road of gold.

But the supreme and final test offered by the anima, or life of the soul, is whether we are up to possessing it. Many fairy tales present this feminine presence in awesome, intimidating, or supernatural terms. To lay out a road entirely of gold is to display an enormous wealth and power. The vital question then becomes: Who can meet and do justice to this magnificence? Who can handle the marvel of true life? Who is equal to its bounty, now at last laid out clearly before us? Probably the one who was able to unlock its secret and set free the marvel in the first place, the youngest son; but certainly not the older sons, whose whole world seems to be comprised of how things affect them. A mind that is caught there will remain there, unable to experience anything beyond itself. The older brothers are therefore self-condemned to failure.

But note the mind of the youngest; because his mind and heart are with the princess, the golden road is as nothing to him. What was an insuperable stumbling block to the egocentric mind vanishes for the mind that is set on the goal of life, that final reunion in which, as the tale says, sorrows will be forgotten. The princess has found the partner who can adequately meet and experience her. These imposing female presences in fairy tales regularly seek such heroes, those who are not put off by the apparent grandeur but can penetrate to the life and love behind it. In our actual relationships, we must beware of projecting onto each other "archetypal" grandeur or power and instead look further, seeking behind this illusion the reality of the person. The kind of love our hero displays can do this. In effect he proves that he loves her and therefore is equal to her wealth and power, and thus he truly wins her. The kingdom that then actually falls to him is a "side-effect" of consistently seeking what is ultimately real. Both the false superiority and the false inferiority of his brothers are proved inadequate and banished from further experience.

Only now is the hero brought back into contact with his father, who, the story says, has "forgiven" him. This is a strange way to put it, since there was clearly nothing to forgive; this wording indicates that our minds must learn to forgive with the presumption that nothing really was done against us. The slate is actually clean and therefore can be seen that way. Grudges are a mistake and a hindrance to ourselves. Again, the third son is exemplary in that he bears absolutely no grudge at any time and is ever ready to be "forgiven," if that is what it takes for reconciliation to occur.

He then lays out to his father all that really happened: the record is set straight now that the real truth has already penetrated consciousness and transformed it. The explanation is not used for vindication or defense; the only real defense is in a change of heart, which has already happened.

So true is all of this that the "enemy" (the older brothers) never needs to be confronted. When the king wishes to punish them, they have already put to sea and are never heard from again. This shows how little it is a question of competition or strife. As the true vision gains ascendancy and comes into its own, the partial, false vision is simply gone. A new state of being brings "all things new," and all the distress of the past is henceforth as if it had never been.

REFERENCE

Hunt, M., trans. 1948. *Grimm's Fairy Tales*. London: Routledge and Kegan Paul.

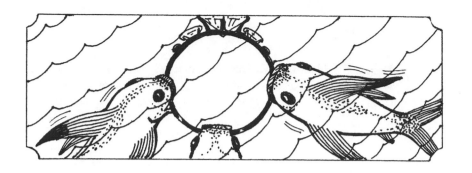

"The White Snake"
A Servant Animus Tale

Geneviève Geer

This Grimm's fairy tale, "The White Snake" (1976, pp. 98–101), provides a rich framework for studying a form of animus energy observed in the psyche of contemporary women. The tale starts "a long time ago" in a kingdom whose king is extremely wise; he appears to be aware of all that is taking place in his kingdom. He also has a strange habit.

The White Snake

E ach night, the king had a covered dish brought to him by his trusty servant. What the dish hid or what the king did with its contents was never revealed. Finally curiosity overcame the servant. He took the dish into his room to find out what it held. When he lifted the cover, he saw a white snake and the moment he looked at it, he could not refrain from cutting a piece of it and eating it. As soon as he had done so, he discovered that he now could understand the language of some birds sitting outside his window.

That very same day, the queen discovered that she was missing her most precious ring. As the servant had the run of the castle, he was immediately suspected. The king let him know that unless he could produce the real thief, he would be considered guilty and executed the following day. His protestations of innocence went unheeded.

Deeply troubled, the servant went outside to think of a way out of his predicament, but his attention was diverted by some ducks chattering alongside a brook. He listened and heard one of them complain of having swallowed a ring that lay under the queen's window.

The servant seized the duck and, taking it to the kitchen, suggested to the cook that it be readied for the spit. The cook agreed and began to prepare the duck; the ring was found in its stomach and the servant was vindicated. The king, to make amends for his suspicion, offered the servant the best place he might want at his court. But the servant turned him down and asked instead for a horse and money; he wanted to travel and see the world. His wishes were granted and he left the kingdom.

On his way, he came to a pond where three fishes caught in some reeds were crying that they were going to perish if they did not get back in the water. He got off his horse and, being kind-hearted, put them back in the water. The fishes thanked him and promised to repay him for saving them.

Later on, as he rode along, he heard a voice at his feet. It was an ant king grumbling that the hooves of the horse were destroying his people. The young man turned the horse away from the anthill and the ant king called out to him that they would remember him, that "one good turn deserves another."

Then he came to a wood, and there he saw two old ravens throwing their young out of the nest and screeching that they were no longer going to feed such good-for-nothing creatures.

The young ravens lay helplessly on the ground, wondering how they were going to survive, being still too young to fly and unable to provide for themselves. The good young man got off his horse and, killing it with his sword, he fed it to the young ravens. The ravens promised him that they would remember him and, like the ants before them, assured him that "one good turn deserves another."

The young man continued his travels on foot to a faraway city. The city was all astir with people and noise; a herald announced to all that the king's daughter wanted a husband but that a suitor must perform a demanding task or perish. Others before had already tried in vain. When the youth saw how beautiful the king's daughter was, he was overwhelmed and declared himself ready to try.

He was taken to the sea and there, before his eyes, a gold ring was tossed into the water. The king then ordered him to retrieve the ring and added that if he returned without it, he would be thrown into the waves until he perished. He sat on the shore, pondering what to do.

Suddenly, three fishes swam toward him; one of them held a mussel in its teeth which it placed at the feet of the young man. It contained the gold ring. The fishes had repaid him by returning the ring to him.

The young man happily went to the king, expecting to be given the princess in marriage. But when the princess saw that he was not as well-born as she, she scorned him and imposed a further task on him. She scattered ten sacks of millet seeds in the garden and told him that they must be picked up and back in the sacks before sunrise.

The youth sat down in the garden but could think of nothing that might save him, and he awaited daybreak and death.

But when the sun rose, he saw all ten sacks filled with the seeds. The ant king had brought thousands and thousands of ants during the night and every seed had been picked up and placed back in the bags.

The princess came down to the garden and was surprised that the young man had succeeded, but she was not ready to give in yet. She announced that he should not be her husband until he had brought her an apple from the Tree of Life. The young man did not know where such a tree existed and started out with no hope of success, but he was prepared to go on walking as long as he possibly could. One night, he came to a wood and settled down under a tree to sleep, and as he rested there, he heard noises in the tree. A golden apple fell into his hand, and three ravens flew down. They were the young ravens he helped save; they heard that he was looking for an apple from the Tree of Life, and they had flown to the end of the world where the Tree stands. They had brought him the apple.

The youth started back happily and took the golden apple to the princess, who could no longer refuse him. They cut the apple in two and ate it together. Then her heart changed and she loved him and "they lived in undisturbed happiness to a great age" (p. 101).

The figure of the servant animus is not a new one in dreams, but it can help throw light on some of the changes in the psyches of contemporary women—changes caused by the societal evolution that has taken place since Jung wrote about the animus. These changes have created new situations for women and engendered new psychological reactions in their psyches. At the time Jung wrote, women's lives were still embedded in the mores of the patriarchy: they were expected, and they expected, to fulfill themselves as wives and mothers. Many of the potentials they had were never developed, and, as often happens to undeveloped talents, they fell into unconsciousness. In a compensatory fashion, the inner masculine element – the animus – became the messenger of lost or yet undiscovered possibilities; it spoke to areas which women had not had the opportunity to explore: activities of the mind, self-assertive behaviors, for instance.

But women are now being trained much in the same way as men and are expected to take their place alongside them in the activities of professional life. Such a profound shift in attitudes has brought about changes in the way women view and experience themselves. Along with these conscious changes, others take place, less visible and often overlooked; changes in the figures which appear in their dreams and which come out of the unconscious to compensate their new conscious attitude.

I have noticed in the past years the appearance of perfectly ordinary men in the dreams of career women, men who do not rank very highly in the social scale. Yet I have also found that these figures – for all of their ordinariness and their humble origin – could become a valuable help to a woman in recovering lost parts of her psyche. A truck driver gives directions to someone who is lost. An electrician fixes broken circuits. A plumber stops an impending flood in a house. A carpenter helps provide shelter.

What their message is and what function they may serve in the psyche of contemporary women will be explored here through the fairy tale "The White Snake."

In it, I will be looking at the princess in the tale as the feminine ego isolated in the father's world and will trace the appearance and growth of the helpful servant animus, at first far removed from her consciousness, eventually coming closer and uniting with her.

As the tale starts, neither the ego nor the servant animus are mentioned. The tale begins "a long time ago" in a kingdom where the king is famed for his wisdom which he seems to acquire through the air. Psychologically speaking, one would say that there is harmony between the ruling principle – the king – and other parts of the psyche. The intuitive knowledge of the king does not appear to be used for selfish power but for wisdom which, one might assume, benefits those whose well-being depends on him.

There is also a mystery about this ruling power; each day the king eats of a dish that is brought to him covered. This would indicate that the king needs more than the usual visible food to sustain himself and that the source of his power is somehow connected with a mystery and a secret. The mystery of the ritual of the dish, and the nature of the king's intuitive knowledge, point to the possibility that his wisdom rests on magical means which may not be revealed to mere mortals. The king then may have indeed held power "a long time ago" when kings were also priests whose authority came from their participation in and familiarity with religious mysteries – mysteries often linked with the cult of the Great Mother (Frazer 1963, chap. 2). In such a situation, the servant would be just that: a servant obedient to an unquestioned and unfathomed if benevolent power.

If one were to think of a woman in a similar situation, one would think of an unquestioning member of a tribe whose consciousness has not yet awakened. Her animus would exist in *participation mystique* with the authority of masculine priestly representatives of the mysteries. Positively, this would amount to a comfortable containment. Negatively, it would be a bond that would hold a woman in unconsciousness.

The tale now turns to the figure of the servant. He is called a "trusty" servant. He is trustworthy and remains so, until curiosity overtakes him and wins out over devotion and trustworthiness. The wish to know, to understand, to discover the secret and to share in the mystery becomes too strong and the servant can no longer resist. He breaks the trust placed in him. No reason is given for this or for the suddenness of his action. It is as if he had been compelled to act by outside forces.

Similarly, there are times in one's own psychological development when one is brought up short by sudden shifts. It seems as if another part of oneself takes over; a sudden remark or a dream will disturb an apparently smooth inner life or a comfortable relationship. Often the disturbance will happen through a compulsive need of the animus to change things, to open closed doors, to uncover secret snake power, to break out of an outlived pattern.

What the servant does is to take the mysterious dish into his room; in other words, he removes something that had belonged to the priestly ruling principle and takes it into his own private psychic space, for his own private use. The servant, in doing so, breaks the unconscious identification with the Self, as it was carried by the king. This he achieves by sacrificing the very quality that characterized him previously: his trustworthiness.

This is an experience that one encounters often during an analysis; it seems that it is the very quality one prizes most in oneself, or that is most admired by others, which suddenly vanishes. It ceases functioning. It is a difficult loss to accept, but one that needs to happen in order for a new consciousness to be born.

Here the change occurs through a break of trust, a disobedient act. Disobedience often is at the source of a coming to consciousness, and its action is usually associated with the early stages of ego formation: the time when the ego moves away from identification with the Self and becomes a separate identity.

Here it appears as if such a process could be initiated by the animus: the animus impulse, in sacrificing the quality that had characterized the personality, begins the long process of separating the ego from the containment in which it existed.

Another effect of the servant's action is to reveal to him the nature of the secret power of the king. The white snake was the source of the king's magic knowledge and power, and the snake points to a subterranean power. Snakes appear in mythology as messengers of the dark regions beneath the earth. They are animals connected with self-renewal; their ability to shed their skins has made them symbols of everlasting life. The snake also appears in mythology as an agent of darkness who may at the same time be the awakener of consciousness. In Greek mythology, it symbolized the power of the Great Mother. The snake in the tale partakes of these various characteristics. It renews itself after being eaten each day, and it tempts the servant into disobedience. Even its color seems to attract attention to the magical quality. The magic and the mystery connected with the tale come through the snake, from under the earth; the transformative power that sets the story in motion rests in this representative of the Mother, and lest it be forgotten, the tale itself takes its name from the snake and its unusual color.

By taking a bite of the snake, the servant acquires the ability to understand the language of animals. In psychological terms, this means that he is now in touch with voices outside the realm of concrete experience; he can hear the messages from the spirit world of the air, the unconscious world of the water, and the chthonic world underground. The servant has acquired the king's magic.

His sudden awareness is like that created by an insight which gives the person who has it an entirely new viewpoint, a separation from the situation which previously contained him or her.

The servant in the story is not suspected of his crime. One would expect the king to know what has happened. If indeed he knows what happens in his kingdom through his magical intuitive powers, he should be able to see what change has taken place in the servant.

One reason this does not take place may be that the servant in the tale stands very close to the king, in a relationship intimate enough to obscure the king's judgment.

The tale, however, says that on the same day the servant took the dish to his room and ate of the snake, the queen lost a very valuable jewel, and the servant was suspected. The sense of betrayal is in the air and the established feminine principle – the queen – becomes aware that something very precious has disappeared. The right person is accused for the right reason but for the wrong deed. One of the effects of the quality of unconscious manifestations is that attempts to interpret them according to logical, conscious ways often lead to wrong conclusions.

For the servant animus, the error proves at first dangerous, and he reacts by withdrawing and trying to think his way out of this dilemma. His help comes from a much more unconscious and instinctual level; as he sits by the brook, he hears ducks talking, and his ability to understand them saves him. The tale here implies that quiet, receptive thinking may be a state necessary to enable one to hear a message from a new, unexpected source. Here the source is the chatter of ducks – those animals who have been linked to the image of the Self because they are equally at home in the air, in the water, and on the earth where they find their nourishment in the mud.

Another reason that the action of the servant is not discovered might be that it was time for a new principle to arise. At such a time, nothing can impede its appearance. The pharaoh's efforts could not do away with Moses, nor did Herod succeed in eradicating the newly born Christ principle.

Looking at the figure of the servant as an animus manifestation, a woman identified with an obedient animus – the servant before his rebellious gesture – would be in danger of remaining unquestioningly in the service of the ruling principle, whichever it might be. She would be contained within the collective and, for her, growth and possible individuality would begin only after some act of independence and some sacrifice of the consciously held sense of her role. The tale brings up the possibility that this can happen through a change in the animus at a level still very far removed from a woman's consciousness. When such a change takes place, a woman may find herself acting and thinking in very new and surprising ways and may wonder where in the world those impulses originated. She may feel both elated and threatened by such mercurial, unexplained reactions.

If such new and unexpected elements are attended to, they will help connect the woman with a different element in her psyche, but the reaction to their appearance is often ambivalent; along with the animus-prompted desire to open things up can go a wish to keep things as they are, to put the lid back on the dish, as if nothing had happened. Such a wish can be born out of a certain fear of change, out of psychological apathy. It can also come from an unconscious pull toward the continuation of the *participation mystique* in which the psyche had existed in a protected state.

These two opposite tendencies often create the atmosphere of confusion which the tale describes. There is confusion and also the threat of a new and autonomous principle. In the tale, it is the servant's possession of the king's secret and power; in everyday life, it might be the new autonomy of a woman.

The servant in the tale does not rush to the king to proclaim his innocence. Along with the magic of the king, he seems to have acquired some of his wisdom; he uses his knowledge and his guile to have the jewel discovered accidentally. Like the king before him, he keeps the source of his information a secret. Innocence has been sacrificed as well as trustworthiness. There is now a new Hermes-like dimension to the energy he represents.

A woman identified with such an aspect of the animus might be manipulative; she might lie and dissemble to ensure her safety and freedom in a collective that she cannot, or will not, think of challenging. This is the way of people who have no authority of their own and must perforce maneuver around the established power.

Such ability to move around obstacles partakes of the wisdom of the snake, which reaches its destination without disturbing the order of things. The first independent steps that women take can have this quality of snakelike movement: telling just enough to satisfy the authorities but subtly altering the spirit of the revelation so as to avoid confrontations. The mercurial servant animus can help them maneuver around obstacles without disturbing them; negatively it can lead them into patterns of dissimulation and dishonesty which will pervade all their relationships and poison them.

After the servant has vindicated himself, the king wants to make amends and offers him more of what he already had. The servant turns down the offer and asks instead for a horse, money, and permission to turn his back on the original container. He wants to discover the world.

A woman identified with this stage of the servant animus might be likely to ask permission of an authority figure or to expect she needed such permission for whatever action she might want to undertake. I have been struck, at times, by the attitude of capable women who expected that their immediate superior would be the one to help promote them. The fact that the superior might be loath to lose a good employee strikes them as unfair and selfish. They see authority figures as having all to say about their success or failure, and they expect benevolent paternal care from them. So they ask for permission. There is, of course, a good deal of worldly wisdom in enlisting the support of a superior as one tries to move forward, but this is not the case with these women. They do not think of themselves as able to negotiate with an authority figure and feel at the mercy of decisions from above.

The danger for a woman at this stage would be to continue in the role of an obedient servant, accepting more of the same instead of moving out into the world, with all the risks and rewards that such an action entails. If she fails to do so, she will easily become embittered by what she sees as the unfairness of society toward women. If she can ask for a horse and money, she can then start out on her journey and risk her comfortable safety for more adventurous endeavors. For her, as for the servant in the tale, the predictable gets left behind as she sets out in the unknown.

The tale now moves away from the original setting and nothing more is heard of the kingdom and its inhabitants. The technique of introducing characters and themes and then abandoning them totally is frequent in fairy tales. It is not a very sophisticated literary device but it creates an effect that is psychologically sound; it points out unmistakably that one era of life is over and that one cannot return to it. The gate of the Garden of Eden is guarded by the angel with a flaming sword; the old ways are done with and one must go forth to discover new ones. In this tale, the change is illustrated by a change in the language itself;

from the moment that he leaves the king, the servant is no longer referred to as "the servant." At first he is called simply "he" and later "a youth." Still later "a handsome youth" by those who pity his fate. The language illustrates well the transformation taking place in him. He has defeated the spirit of inertia and is actively participating with his destiny. His requests are for forms of energy that will make his entrance into the world easier: a horse for mobility and ease of travel, and money, a form of energy that can so easily be transformed into other needed facilities.

In the same way, a woman who has been able to break away from the containment of a servantlike attitude and to start on her own journey will begin to experience her masculine energy in a new and more positive way. Although it is still alien and very removed from her ego, it is moving toward consciousness.

Along his way, the young man comes to the rescue of three different sets of animals. His first actions—freeing three fishes and sparing an anthill—are triggered by the fact that he understands the animals' complaints and heeds them. These first two gestures are small enough and accomplished at little expense to him.

The fishes are water-dwelling animals; as such they represent thoughts or feelings guessed at through the ever-moving surface of the water. If one looks upon water as the unconscious, fishes are unconscious contents that spontaneously appear; they float almost to full view only to melt back into the depths (von Franz 1977, p. 150). In the tale, the fishes are released back into their natural environment instead of being stifled in the reeds. Similarly, there are times in an analysis when certain contents come up from the unconscious in the form of dream images or characters in guided imagination, and which evoke no affective response in the analysand. If these images can be evoked and perhaps concretized in drawings or sandtray pictures, their energy can be released to swim freely in the unconscious and eventually return some valuable treasure to consciousness. In the tale, the fishes are released by the action of the animus, pointing to the dynamic power of the animus working at a deeply unconscious level.

The second set of animals is a colony of ants. These insects live in the earth in highly organized matriarchal societies, and they are identified with the notions of work and industry. They appear in fairy tales and myths as helping the heroine in a moment of need: they sort the grain for the beautiful Wassilissa and for Psyche in the Greek myth. Their diligence is put at the service of a new feminine principle suffering the attacks of a negative feminine force. One might say that there are times when industry, attention to detail, and small but precise tasks are the qualities needed to help a new principle survive the attacks of the negative feminine.

In the tale, the young man saves the ants by going slightly out of his way and avoiding them, a thoughtful but not demanding action.

It is the third encounter that throws a different light on his nature. The young man responds to the crisis of the young ravens in a most unusual way; he does not attempt to reason with the parents, nor does he take the young ravens with him. Instead he kills his horse, sacrificing it to feed the young birds.

Ravens are birds whose significance is important in mythology in general and in this tale in particular. They are sacred birds connected with the creation of the world; they are the bringers of light in American Indian myths (von Franz 1972, pp. 20-25). European mythology has a more ambivalent view of them: they are still sacred birds, messenger birds – the birds of Wotan and Hermes – but they are often placed under a curse. Yet they can also be messengers from God; ravens were sent to feed Elijah in the desert. In folklore, they are considered to be portents of evil; if ravens come and settle near a house, it is thought to mean that a death is coming there.

In Jungian psychology, the raven is representative of the alchemical *nigredo*, the blackening belonging to the *mortificatio* of which Edinger says that it is the most negative operation in alchemy. It has to do with darkness, defeat, torture, mutilation, death, and rotting (1981, p. 25). Its hallmark is the color black.

The raven, in its blackness and in its function as a carrion eater, carries the symbol of that state of psychological despair which is so like a death. Jung says of the stage of blackness that it is a necessary state before transformation can take place in an operation that repeats the admonition of Christ, that lest the grain dies it shall not bear fruit (Jung 1955-1956, par. 733).

Psychologically speaking, saving young ravens from death would mean encouraging a nascent state of *nigredo* to grow and flourish. It would be the equivalent of staying with a depression and allowing it to deepen in order to experience the message that it has to deliver. Such a choice is a difficult one to make, as one is tempted to avoid pain and to search for easy solutions. It is the human tendency to avoid pain that makes the action of the young man in the tale all the more unusual. His choice shows a connection with a wisdom that comes from a source deeper than what one expects from an ego attitude, a wisdom born out of the Self which values unexpected and outwardly negative messages and nurtures their need to be addressed, just as it welcomes positive ones.

For a woman it is often an animus-generated reaction that places her in the situation the tale describes: that of fostering the growth of ambivalent new elements which she might consciously prefer to avoid. When she reacts out of the unconscious, her animus tends to take over and entangles her in new and often difficult situations which might be quite detrimental to her outwardly, but from which she can learn and grow a great deal if she will sit with them and integrate the messages that they bring her.

The action of the young man puts the tale in a context different from that of heroic, patriarchal tales where a sacrifice on the part of the hero takes place either to save an anima-like feminine figure, or to allow him to continue on toward some specific conquest. The young man is willing to sacrifice what appears to be the higher for the sake of what is lower. He sacrifices the horse that had been given to him by the king, and which represented a way of fast and comfortable travel. It also represented far more than that in the society of that time: from the Latin word *caballus* we now have the words *cavalry*, *cavalier*, *chivalry*, etc., all words associated with masculine nobility, pride, and heroic deeds. A man on horseback is highly visible; he stands out over the crowd and cuts a very different figure from a man on foot — humble and close to the earth. One cannot but wonder what kind of a reception the young man would have had from the princess in the next kingdom if he had arrived riding a horse from a king's stable.

Psychologically speaking, his actions are prompted not by what one would call the reality principle, but by another set of values that differ profoundly from those of worldly wisdom.

A woman identified with the type of animus energy that the young man represents at this point might spontaneously adopt a rather idealistic attitude. She might also be quite amazed at other people's reactions to her actions and to her opinions: "This is not the way the world works" and "Things are just not like that" are remarks that might come her way. Women who are beginning to react out of their own values are frequently wounded by such remarks and are led to question their whole view of life and of themselves. Their view—one could say the view of the servant masculine in them—is that it might take the life of a horse to protect what is weak and feeble even if it is a black raven. It is difficult to stand up for the Artemis quality of protecting all that is young and in need. Too often a woman will back down and accept the world's view of what is right and real, over her own deeply felt values. That can be the beginning of her repudiation of her own inner nonheroic masculine as wrong, while in truth it is not wrong but different from the collective judgment of the patriarchy.

If she can relate consciously to this type of animus energy, she will be sensitive to the need of others, but it might be at the expense of her own comfort, and the instinctive and intuitive nature of her actions might leave her very vulnerable to attacks from the more logical, practical viewpoint of others.

On a deeper psychological level, the sacrifice of the horse symbolizes a sacrifice of libido; the image of the hero and his horse is that of a man and the subordinate sphere of animal instinct. The sacrifice of the horse to feed the ravens is a sacrifice of raw energy to a far more sacred and complex symbol of psychic energy; it is the sacrifice of libido freely offered to nurture dark, sacred fledglings.

A servant animus in a woman might sacrifice on her behalf what to a more conscious view would be a greater good. If the woman identifies with such an animus, she might become "the martyr," complaining and burdensome to her environment. But if she can remain conscious and psychologically attuned to the messages that her animus brings her, she will be connected to a different spiritual dimension, one which will allow sacrifice to take place without bitterness or hope of reward. It will also allow her to familiarize herself with the source of the power of such animus energy.

The action of the young man does not relate him to the heroic tradition; it finds its roots in the Mother with her rhythms of birth, sacrifice, and death, her closeness to the earth, her profoundly different ordering of values—an ordering that often seems illogical and erroneous if judged by collective patriarchal standards. The relationship of the young man to the powers of the Mother is not that of a son/lover but that of a servant and a messenger between her domain and that of the patriarchal world. The energy he represents comes from the chthonic sources of snake power. For a woman such animus energy is her link to the world of the Mother and her messenger from it.

After his third encounter, he travels on foot for a long time before reaching the kingdom where he will meet the princess. The servant animus, messenger from the mother world still has a long journey before connecting with the feminine ego, much as at times during an analysis an outburst of spiritual and psychological insights will be followed by a long period of plodding along with seemingly very little meaning to one's journey.

As he reaches the town, the youth hears an announcement: the king's daughter wants a husband. This marks the first appearance of the feminine ego in the tale. It has up to now existed quite apart from the unconscious energy coming to meet with it.

The little that is known of the young woman is that she is designated in the tale by a title symbolic of her relationship to her father. Psychologically speaking, to refer to her as the king's daughter is to call attention to a possession by the father energy, the father animus. Her situation there parallels that of the servant at the beginning of the tale, who was defined by his relationship to the king; she is, as he was, servant to another power and her identity is obtained through another.

There is, however, a profound difference: in the first part of the tale, the animus energy was so far removed from the conscious ego of the princess that there was no way for it to become available to her. In the kingdom of her father, although she is still held by the power of her identification with him, she is an active participant in her destiny. She wants to make contact with a new form of masculine energy, one better suited to her. The tale says that she, the princess, wants a husband; psychologically speaking, she is asking for a connection to her own animus energy and thinks of herself as ready to do so. Her later concerns will not be with having to join in a union with someone else, but with the nature of the person with whom she is to be joined.

The young man is dazzled by her beauty and agrees to undertake any trial in order to win the princess. Women who so often feel attacked and demeaned by the negative animus are rarely aware that it can also be the loving suitor ready to undertake daring deeds to free them from their princesslike isolation. Many react to such figures in their dreams with the same kind of disdain the princess displays in the tale. It is too close, too easily obtained, and certainly not grand enough to be valued.

Others, if they identify with that aspect of the servant animus, may find themselves offering their services to some attractive cause or other and may get caught in a savior complex for which they will receive very little thanks.

The deed required of the young man, apparently impossible to accomplish, is to retrieve a gold ring from the sea, or die. The ring as a circle is a symbol of the Self: infinite and yet finite. In its form and in its substance, it unites feminine and masculine elements in a single object symbolic of union between the sexes (von Franz 1970, p. 8).

The king throws this golden symbol in the deepest waters of the unconscious and bids the young man retrieve it. The youth reacts to the request in the way he had reacted to the accusation of having stolen the queen's ring; he simply sits and despairs. It is as if none of the experiences he has gone through have taught him to count on the powers that he has.

Women identified with this aspect of the animus will be plagued by what a woman once referred to as "psychological anorexia." It is as if they do not absorb and get nourished by their own past experiences and their own achievements. One has to keep reminding them that they are good, that they are capable, that they hold the key to solving their own problems. Their achievements, their ability do not help build up their self-esteem or their sense of self. They look to a savior outside themselves, quite unaware that the savior exists within their own psyche.

If, on the other hand, they can become aware of such a tendency in themselves, they may begin to learn that for them a solution will at times come out of moments of doubt and insecurity. Once they are familiar with such a pattern, they will no longer be its victim, but will adapt to its cyclicality, recognize it, and make use of its death and rebirth nature.

As is often the case, the answer to the life and death situation in which the young man finds himself is solved by an answer from the unconscious. The fishes come to his rescue and return the ring to him.

Up to now, the story has followed a pattern often found in fairy tales: an unprepossessing young man succeeds where others have failed and wins the princess. At this point, however, there is a change; when the princess perceives that the young man is not her equal in birth, she scorns him and requires him to perform another task. The princess, in doing this, moves out of passive identification of herself as the king's daughter and becomes actively indentified with her princesshood as something of great worth. It is at the time that she becomes outwardly free from her father's orders – defying the agreement that whosoever retrieved the ring would win her – that she takes on collective persona values. She falls into the situation described by Hilda Biswanger when she speaks of "the animus climbing the steps of the persona," and isolating the woman behind a wall built by the prestige- and persona-minded animus (Biswanger 1965, p. 9). The princess has internalized the values of birth and rank with which she has lived, and she is rigidly held prisoner by their tyranny. It is often when one begins to make conscious ego choices that the danger becomes great of unconsciously adopting parental values that seem to have been left behind.

If, like the women mentioned earlier, the princess has acquired no inner sense of her capability and strength, she will automatically reject a connection with something less than visibly heroic. Her sense of identity will come from persona reassurance and she will feel that a servantlike youth cannot provide her with the power and the visibility she craves. One sees this played out quite often in women who come to analysis and try to sort out the conflicts they have in their relationships and in their careers; at some point in their analysis, many exclaim with horror, "But if I did this, I would be just ordinary," or else, "I would have just an ordinary life." To them, "ordinary" is equated with mediocrity, failure, and with total stifling. It seems that only the grandiose will suffice to offset what the analyst can perceive as their deep sense of insecurity.

The princess does not want to accept the young man as a mate and sets out to destroy him and remain in her father's world. The young man, however, performs the tasks she imposes on him. After winning her from her father, he wins her from her persona-animus possession. He does not question her whims, but is willing to try and please her. The type of animus energy that he represents is often unnoticed, while the painful punitive effects of the negative animus are stressed. Women themselves tend to take this willing animus for granted, to undervalue and overlook its contributions.

The young man in the tale has to perform tasks that are both feminine and masculine in nature. The first one imposed by the princess is to gather up seeds. The motif of seeds in fairy tales usually appears in the context of sorting out seeds, a task that has to do with discrimination and that is usually performed by women. In this tale, there is no discrimination; there is not even any point to the whole task. The spilling of seeds just to have them gathered up again has a wanton quality to it, unlike the separating of good and bad seeds. Because there is no point to the task, it leaves one with a feeling of wrong thinking on the part of the princess, almost as if she had heard of tasks imposed and was applying them out of context. One can speculate that some major element in her psychology has been left untouched, uneducated. The absence of any mention of a queen in that kingdom implies that there has been no feminine influence in her life. She has not been taught the importance of relatedness, and she has been left to fend for herself in maladapted ways, mixing indiscriminately masculine and feminine values and methods.

Similarly, many contemporary women have been steeped in what Neumann described as "the archetypically conditioned culture canon in the West that enforces masculine patriarchal development on every child whether it be masculine or feminine" (1959, p. 78). They have not known a feminine viewpoint and tend to identify with masculine and patriarchal values. What has been sacrificed is their femininity; they learned to live in the clear-headed world of the paternal logos, but they became cut off from the world of the Mother. When they encounter the demands of the feminine, they often react in the way Emma Jung described in her essay on the animus. She spoke of professional women whose achievements were disturbed by feminine longings with which they had difficulty coping; then, she said, "their dilemma is similar to that of a man with respect to the anima; that is, these women, too, are confronted with the difficulty of sacrificing what, to a certain degree, is a higher development, or at least a superiority," in order to accept their feminine side (E. Jung 1957, p. 41).

This may also explain, at least in part, the fact that it is a masculine messenger who tries to reconnect the woman with her feminine side: in the psychology of the puella, it takes a masculine figure to force her to pay attention to a problem to be addressed, because it carries perforce more authority that a feminine one. Seen in another light, the masculine figure is explained by Jung in the *Visions Seminars* when he said that "in a situation where the contents are too far from consciousness, so that consciousness is unable to realize them, then those contents are enacted by the animus, *as if it were the animus that was concerned with them*" (Jung 1976, p. 76; emphasis mine). The animus as agent of the Self makes it its task to reconnect the conscious feminine ego with the parts that have become lost. In this case the parts that have been lost have to do with the realm of the feminine, the domain of the Mother.

The young man performs the task with the help of the ants; small instinctual beings who appear to defend a new principle from the attacks of a negative one. This time, the new principle has to do with relatedness and is carried by the masculine servant animus, while the princess tries to destroy it.

The next task, the quest for the golden apple, is a masculine heroic quest and a difficult one. The youth goes off through many kingdoms until he reaches a wood, and there, exhausted, he falls asleep. Woods "where vision is limited, where one loses one's way, where wild animals and unexpected dangers may be present, are a symbol of the unconscious," as is, of course, being asleep (von Franz 1970, p. 11). It is in this completely unconscious state that he receives the apple from the three ravens. The image here underlines once more that source of his strength lies in the unconscious, and that he has to experience himself as overwhelmed before a spontaneous manifestation will come to save him.

The ravens bring him the golden apple from the Tree of Life which is found at the end of the world. The Tree of Life calls forth the image of the Garden of Eden in which it grew. In the tale, it grows at the end of the world. The fruit — the golden apple from the Tree of Life — is a symbol of the Self (Jung 1954, par. 404), and this treasure, which is hard to attain, is bestowed upon the youth by the winged, sacred messengers who can go to the end of the world and return. The youth, in bringing the golden apple to the princess, proves himself to be the agent of the Self who gives back to the feminine ego the ability to live in "undisturbed happiness."

From the point of view of the princess, the tale would go this way: she has lived for years in an environment deprived of feminine influence; feminine values of relatedness and personal contacts have fallen into darkness and become negative; she is totally identified — in puella fashion — with her father's values and does not even know how to impose a feminine task. Yet she also displays the desire to make contact with another human being; the tale says that she wants to have a husband — a personal counterpart of herself. No one has taught her how to go about this as there has been no feminine influence. There has been no real logos guidance from her father either; he does not attempt to make her live up to her commitment to the young man, after the return of the ring. She has to make her own decisions, including deciding what she wants, and how she is going to go about it. She feels free until the servant animus catches up with her in his wish to be united with her. The unknown element that has been developing away from her consciousness is now asking to be taken into her consciousness and integrated. Like any new element, it disturbs the homeostasis of the psyche, and at first the reaction of the conscious psyche is negative.

But the princess also has a deeper connection to her own needs; despite her negative attitude to the youth, she asks him to provide her with the golden apple from the Tree of Life. Consciously she might have hoped that her wish be his undoing, but what she has requested is also a gift symbolic of a union other than that between man and woman; it is the fruit of the successful completion of the opus, in other words, of a spiritual conjunction between masculine and feminine. In imposing the nearly impossible task on the youth, the princess is also asking the animus to help reconnect her with the living sources of the Self.

Had the hero who returned the ring been a prince or a knight, the princess might have been content to accept him without any further trial. Psychologically speaking, this would have meant for her that her sense of self would have still been carried by another and not integrated into her own psyche. The very character of the servant, because of its more humble traits, forced the princess to accept a part of the psyche which at first did not appear to be worthy of her. Much like shadow contents, servant animus energy forces the ego to reassess its view of itself. It also forces it to a more realistic and therefore more solid stance.

The young man of the tale is not only a servant; his origins in the world of the mother make him a connection to the feminine. And for a father's daughter, the acceptance of a more shadowy feminine side echoes Emma Jung's words of the difficulty in accepting a "lower," "more feminine" aspect of oneself.

Many young women today are in this situation. Their lives are different from those of previous generations; they have no one to turn to for guidance in their decisions. They have to set their own values for themselves, and they have to learn to set a value *on* themselves. Anyone who has had to name a salary scale or set a fee has done just that. Women have had no tradition passed on to them to help them make such decisions.

This lack of tradition makes it difficult for them to make clear, factual decisions out of the ego. They become anxious or fearful, and their anxiety can trigger a lowering of consciousness. At such times, the animus takes over either in an exalted way, and the woman will feel indignant at not being valued enough, or in an obedient servant fashion, which will leave her feeling inferior and lacking a sense of her unique worth. Either way, she will be unable to separate the objective view of her worth in the marketplace from that of her sense of self-worth. Such experiences will leave her feeling bewildered and victimized. At times like these, help sometimes appears, quite unexpectedly, from another aspect of the animus; one that is very close to the woman herself. Emma Jung has called this a function of the personal unconscious of the woman but whose origins also link it to the collective unconscious as a representative of the Mother (E. Jung 1967, p. 27). This energy is there to serve and help her if she will let it. Usually, once its task is accomplished, it will disappear, leaving the woman now able to act on her own.

If this is so, one might ask what makes it so difficult for a woman to accept this masculine principle within her. There are reasons for a woman's reluctance to take these servantlike images seriously.

One lies in the ambivalent nature of the servant himself. On one hand, he is unaware of his powers and loses confidence easily; on the other hand, he succeeds where others fail and loses neither heart nor patience, but remains faithful to the wishes of the princess. A woman might fear finding herself caught in the negative aspects of this energy; she might fear that help might not come from her moments of discouragement and that she might remain depressed and helpless.

Another reason lies in the unheroic figure of the young man. A woman who feels insecure and afraid will wish for a man of strength and authority to offset her sense of weakness; a servant who becomes despondent may not seem like the right kind of support for her either in a real man or in an inner figure. Women have also been influenced by the masculine ideal that exists in the West; it is an ideal of brains, brawn, and self-confidence. Women – although many of them claim that they would prefer men to be more sensitive – have internalized these Western values. All too often, they want masculine figures that stand for success in the world. The qualities that make a man successful are rarely those that will also make him sensitive. A servant inner figure would not bring a sense of success and authority to them.

Socially, of course, a humble servant would not be the most interesting escort one might want. Even when dealing with dream figures, the tendency remains to make value judgments. Mostly though, the reaction of women may be due to a much deeper problem. The servant is a messenger from the world of the feminine; for many a woman today, this is an unknown and much feared world. The world of the feminine is the one that they see as having enslaved their mothers and against which they struggle. They fear its lack of clarity, its illogical demands, its biological cycles. They desperately want to face the light and turn their backs on the shadowy side of their nature. A servant figure, appearing as it does from that realm, frightens them, and they try to ignore it and escape its attentions. For many women, to accept that side of themselves feels like a threat: the threat of being swallowed up by unconsciousness. They have won their newly found conscious stand at a price, and they dread losing it entirely if they so much as question it. Any messenger from the darker regions appears to be an enemy.

If, however, they can overcome their fear and befriend him, they will learn from him that masculine and feminine values need not be enemies. They will find their personality enriched by the ability to accept both modes and to move freely from one to the other. They will experience the fulfillment of an inner union with an inner figure that values their femininity and that is at their service. A relationship with such a figure can do much to bring an "undisturbed" sense of self to a woman.

REFERENCES

Biswanger, Hilda. 1965. Ego, animus and persona in the feminine psyche, *Harvest* 11 (1965): 1–15.
Edinger, Edward F. 1981. Psychotherapy and alchemy: VI mortificatio. *Quadrant* 14:23–45.
Frazer, Sir James George. 1963. *The Golden Bough*. New York: Macmillan Publishing Co., Inc.
Grimm, the Brothers. 1976. *The Complete Grimm's Fairy Tales*. New York: Pantheon Books.
Jung, C. G. 1952. *Symbols of Transformation. CW*, vol. 5. Princeton, N.J.: Princeton University Press, 1956.
_____. 1954. The philosophical tree. *CW* 13:251–349. Princeton, N.J.: Princeton University Press, 1967.

_____. 1955-1956. *Mysterium Coniunctionis. CW*, vol. 14. Princeton, N.J.: Princeton University Press, 1963.

_____. 1976. *The Visions Seminars*. Zurich: Spring Publications.

Jung, Emma. 1957. *Animus and Anima*. Carl F. Baynes and Hildegard Nagel, trans. Zurich: Spring Publications.

_____. 1967. Letter to E. P. Kotschnig. *Inward Light* 30, 72 (1967): 27-29.

Neumann, Eric. 1959. The psychological stages of feminine development. *Spring*, pp. 63-97.

von Franz, Marie-Louise. 1970. *Interpretation of Fairy Tales*. New York: Spring Publications.

_____. 1972. *Creation Myths*. Zurich: Spring Publications.

_____. 1977. *Individuation in Fairy Tales*. Zurich: Spring Publications.

About the Authors

Volume 1

Jole Cappiello McCurdy, M.D., was a specialist in neurology and psychiatry, a graduate of the C. G. Jung Institute of Rome (CIPA), and assistant professor of psychiatry at the University of Pennsylvania.

Julia M. Jewett is an ordained minister in the United Church of Christ, a pastoral therapist and member of the American Association of Pastoral Counselors, a diplomate Jungian analyst affiliated with the Chicago Society of Jungian Analysts, a wife, mother and grandmother. She has a private practice in Wilmette, Illinois, and a special interest in women's poetry, art, and spirituality.

Irene Gad, M.D., worked as a research scientist in classical conditioning and psychopharmacology at the Romanian Academy of Science before emigrating to France in 1960. She came to the U.S. in 1965, earned her M.A. in psychology and a Ph.D. in human sexuality, and taught experimental psychology and human sexuality at the College of St. Thomas, St. Paul, Minnesota. She received her diploma from the C. G. Jung Institute in Zurich and has since conducted a private practice in the Washington, D.C., area. She is currently working on a book, *Tarot and Individuation.*

Anne Baring received her M.A. in modern history and published *The One Work: A Journey Towards the Self.* She worked as a dress designer and ran her own shop in London. In 1985 she became a member of the Association of Jungian Analysts, London, and the International Association of Jungian Analysts. Her most recent book is *The Myth of the Goddess: Evolution of an Image* with Jules

Cashford. She is currently writing and practicing as a Jungian analyst in England. Married to artist Robin Baring, she has a daughter.

Lena B. Ross, Ph.D., is a Jungian analyst, trained at the C. G. Jung Institute of New York, with a private practice in Manhattan, where she is on the faculty of the Center for Analytical Perspectives. She is interested in the psychological significance of disobedience in the development of the psyche, the theme of *To Speak or Be Silent: The Paradox of Disobedience in the Lives of Women* (forthcoming, Chiron), a collection of essays on literature and disobedience from around the world, which she is editing.

Robert Bly has published a number of books of poetry, the most recent of which is his collected prose poems, *What Have I Ever Lost By Dying?* He has also translated poems and versions of many European and Asian poets, including Antonio Machado, Georg Trakl, Rainer Maria Rilke, Kabir, Mirabai, and Rumi. His first full-length book of prose, *Iron John,* includes poems, stories, mythological comment, and social commentary. He lives in Minnesota.

Lionel Corbett is a Jungian analyst in private practice in Santa Fe, New Mexico.

Kathy Rives is a psychiatrist in private practice in Santa Fe, New Mexico, and a candidate at the C. G. Jung Institute of Chicago.

Kathrin Asper is an analyst in private practice and a lecturer, training analyst, and member of the Curatorium at the C. G. Jung Institute in Kusnacht-Zurich. Her university studies cover language, literature, and education, and she has published many articles on analytical psychology. Author of several books in German, her English works include *The Inner Child in Dreams* and *Abandonment and Self-Estrangement.*

Ladson Hinton, M.A., M.D., completed his graduate studies in philosophy at the University of Arkansas, in medicine at Washington University, and psychiatric training at Stanford. A graduate of the C. G. Jung Institute of San Francisco, he has been on its faculty and was associate clinical professor of psychiatry at Stanford. He is currently in private practice in Seattle and a founding member and president of Jungian Analysts North Pacific. He has lectured and written on fairy tales, the psychology of humor, animal symbols in myth and dream, and the fool archetype.

Lucille Klein, M.A., NCPsyA, is a nurse practitioner and a diplomate Jungian analyst in private practice in Evanston and Matteson, Illinois. Born in Mississippi and educated there and in Tennessee, she then joined the U.S. Naval Nurse Corps. Much of her early childhood was spent listening to tales, which was the start of her interest in myths and fairy tales. She is currently an instructor and chair of the Analyst Training Program at the C. G. Jung Institute of Chicago.

Volume 2

Frances M. Parks, Ph.D., was born and raised in Oklahoma, delighted and sometimes frightened by troll stories and other myths and fairy tales. In college, her mother introduced her to the work of C. G. Jung, which led to her training at the C. G. Jung Institute at Zurich, receiving her diploma in 1986. She currently lives and practices in Bethesda, Maryland, where she shares troll stories with her daughter.

Caroline Stevens, Ph.D., NCPsyA, studied in Zurich and Chicago, where she received her diploma in 1985. She conducts a private practice and teaches in the analyst training and public education programs at the C. G. Jung Institute of Chicago. She is vice president of the Chicago Society of Jungian Analysts and a member of the American Board for Accreditation in Psychoanalysis. Her theoretical concerns center around an understanding of women's individuation and the philosophical underpinnings of Jungian thought.

Claire Douglas is a clinical psychologist and an advanced candidate at the C. G. Jung Institute of New York. She is a 1991–1992 Bunting Fellow at Radcliffe College and the author of *The Woman in the Mirror: Analytical Psychology and the Feminine* and *Translate This Darkness: The Life of Christiana Morgan*. She is the editor of Princeton University Press's new and complete edition of C. G. Jung's *The Visions Seminars*. She conducts a private practice and lectures on contemporary issues in women's psychology.

T. J. Kapacinskas, J.D., NCPsyA, received his Jungian training in Zurich, graduating in 1972. He subsequently became a founding member of the Inter-Regional Society of Jungian Analysts and of the C. G. Jung Institute of Chicago. He is presently a training analyst at the Chicago Institute and has a private practice in Evanston, Illinois, and South Bend, Indiana, where he lives with his wife, Judith Robert, and their newborn daughter.

Judith A. Robert, Ph.D., is a graduate of the Northwestern University Counseling Psychology program and currently a candidate in the C. G. Jung Institute of Chicago. She is a practiced astrologer as well as a therapist in private practice in South Bend, Indiana. Both she and her husband give workshops and classes on fairy tales.

Marilyn L. Matthews, M.D., is a psychiatrist and Jungian analyst with a private practice in Santa Fe and Albuquerque, New Mexico. She has taught classes in Milwaukee, Chicago, and Santa Fe on various subjects, including envy and competition between women, power and the shadow of power, and women's visionary experiences. For the past several years, she has served as the training coordinator for the New Mexico branch of the IRSJA.

Ronald T. Curran, Ph.D., is an associate professor at the University of Pittsburgh and a psychotherapist at the Pittsburgh Center for Psychotherapy and Psychoanalysis and at Family Resources, a United Way agency specializing in the treatment of physical and sexual abuse. At present, he is a candidate in the Inter-Regional Society of Jungian Analysts. Among his publications are two edited collections, *Witches, Wraiths & Warlocks* and *Witches, Water Spirits & Fairies*. He teaches courses at the C. G. Jung Educational Center of Pittsburgh and at Western Psychiatric Institute and Clinic, where he lectures on Jungian psychology to residents in the Advanced General Psychiatry Literature Seminar. His most recent paper is "Rescuing Kali from the 'Indians': Culture, Archetype, and Primordial Unconscious."

Lee Zahner-Roloff, Ph.D., is professor emeritus of Northwestern University. Presently, he is an analyst in private practice in Evanston, Illinois, and training analyst at the C. G. Jung Institute of Chicago.

Alfred Collins, Ph.D., is a clinical psychologist in private practice in Anchorage, Alaska. He also holds a doctorate in Indian studies from the University of Texas and has done research in Sanskrit at the University of Madras. His published papers bridge the two fields and aim to develop or uncover an "Indian self psychology."

David L. Hart, Ph.D., is a Jungian analyst in private practice in Arlington, Massachusetts. Trained at the C. G. Jung Institute in Zurich, his love of fairy tales goes back to his diploma thesis on the challenge of the anima in fairy tales. Author of many published articles, many in *Psychological Perspectives,* he looks forward to producing a collection focusing on fairy tales.

Geneviève Geer, born in Paris, was educated in France and the U.S., where she received her B.A., certificate in psychiatric rehabilitation, and M.S.W. She is a graduate of the C. G. Jung Institute of New York and is at present a diplomate in clinical social work. She is a member of the faculty of the New York Institute, where she has supervisory and teaching duties, and is president of the New York Association for Analytical Psychology. Her articles have appeared in *Quest* and *Quadrant.*